a
sideways
look
at
clouds

a
sideways
look
at
clouds

maria
mudd
ruth

MOUNTAINEERS
BOOKS

Mountaineers Books is the publishing division of The Mountaineers, an organization founded in 1906 and dedicated to the exploration, preservation, and enjoyment of outdoor and wilderness areas.

MOUNTAINEERS BOOKS   1001 SW Klickitat Way, Suite 201, Seattle, WA 98134
800.553.4453, www.mountaineersbooks.org

Printed in Canada
Distributed in the United Kingdom by Cordee, www.cordee.co.uk
20 19 18 17   1 2 3 4 5

Copy editor: Chris Dodge
Cover and book design: Jen Grable
Endsheet illustration: Anna-Lisa Notter, www.annalisanotter.com
All photographs by the author unless otherwise credited.
Symbols at the start of each chapter are used in meteorological charts and reports to indicate cloud types. Cloud illustrations on endsheets reflect the approximate altitudinal relationship of the ten main types of clouds; these are graphic representations only and not intended for identification purposes.

Library of Congress Cataloging-in-Publication Data
Names: Ruth, Maria Mudd.
Title: A sideways look at clouds / Maria Mudd Ruth.
Description: Seattle, WA : Mountaineers Books, [2017] | Includes index.
Identifiers: LCCN 2017012746 (print) | LCCN 2017009778 (ebook) | ISBN
   9781680511185 (trade paper) | ISBN 9781680511192 (ebook)
Subjects: LCSH: Clouds. | Atmosphere. | Cloud physics.
Classification: LCC QC921 .R93 2017 (ebook) | LCC QC921 (print) | DDC
   551.57/6—dc23
LC record available at https://lccn.loc.gov/2017012746

Mountaineers Books titles may be purchased for corporate, educational, or other promotional sales, and our authors are available for a wide range of events. For information on special discounts or booking an author, contact our customer service at 800-553-4453 or mbooks@mountaineersbooks.org.

♲ Printed on recycled paper

ISBN (hardcover): 978-1-68051-118-5
ISBN (ebook): 978-1-68051-119-2

For my guys

Contents

PROLOGUE

a guide to the sky

I learned the names of the clouds when I was forty-eight years old—too old, it seemed, to be learning something I should have memorized long ago with my multiplication tables and state capitals. I was not in a classroom at the time or reading a book about the weather but standing in the dim hallway of a neighbor's house, jangling my car keys, irked.

The neighbor had called me earlier that October morning for a last-minute ride to the train station. When I arrived at her house, she was just starting to pack her bags. She was running late and I was in rush. I had set aside that particular morning to settle on the subject for my next book—a decision I had been agonizing over for too long. Away from my desk, I was certain I was missing the appearance of my erstwhile muse.

I stood in her front hall and called out the time every few minutes. I cleared my throat histrionically. I asked about a later train. When this failed to hasten our departure, I waited some more—badly, impatiently, loudly. I wanted to be a patient person, a good neighbor, and a productive writer, but I was failing miserably at all three. I closed my eyes and breathed deeply. I shifted my weight from one foot to the other. I rolled my shoulders. I stretched my neck. I turned my head slowly to the right and then the left. That's when I saw them—the clouds—dozens of them, just two feet away.

They were luscious, dappled, upswept, wind-whipped, storm-tossed, and so full of energy that they seemed more like trapped, living clouds than photographs. But there they were, in neat rows, confined in four-by-four-inch squares on a poster pinned to the hall-closet door.

The clouds sprawled across skies, dwarfing the landscapes beneath them. Mountain ranges cowered, forests seemed stunted, skyscrapers and church steeples appeared puny.

At the top of the poster was an assertive title: *A Guide to the Sky*. I turned on the hallway light and stepped closer to the door. I scanned all thirty clouds but did not see the names of the clouds I knew—"mare's tails," "thunderheads," "mackerel skies." I recognized some of the cloud shapes but could not guess their names—their scientific Latin names—Cirrus, Cumulus, Stratus, and others that appeared beneath each photo.

My ignorance appalled and intrigued me. Were these not the kinds of clouds I had always lived under? Were these not the cloud names that appeared in every science book for children and on every classroom water-cycle poster or weather chart I had laid my eyes on over the years? I could not recall when or where I had learned these names—if I ever had. Clouds seemed like strangers now, after too many years of not saying their names, of barely glancing at them and only then if they were spectacular. Even after moving to the Pacific Northwest—to the cloud-covered city of Olympia, Washington—I hadn't given clouds the time of day. I had certainly had no interest in being on a first-name basis with them.

But as I stood there in the hallway that morning, the clouds grabbed me and would not let go. I could not take my eyes off the cloud poster. Suddenly, waiting became floating.

"Stratus: The sky is low, the air is damp when Stratus covers the sky. Stratus like this occurs when the air is mostly calm. When the droplet spectrum is broad, misty drizzle can form, making it difficult to ride a bike if you wear glasses."

I could not recall seeing such clouds or noticing their presence on my glasses.

"Altocumulus perlucidus: This cloud often produces memorable sunrises or sunsets. Though traces of ice may be present, this thin cloud is usually composed solely of droplets in small, honeycomb-like cloudlets. In patches, it suggests storms are far away."

How could I turn my back on these clouds and on the invitation to look up?
(A Guide to the Sky, 8th edition, © Art Rangno, 2000)

I wasn't aware that clouds could have two names.

"Cumulonimbus mammatus: Thunder grouses among grotesque, downward-moving bulges of cloud (usually composed of ice crystals) that form mammatus pouches. These are found in the dissipating portions of thunderstorms."

Though this poster appeared to be scientific, to me the captions read like poetry. As did the large block of text at the bottom:

> When compared to the earth's size, the layer of atmosphere in which all clouds form is no thicker than the leather cover on a softball. Within this fragile layer is a myriad of continuously evolving forms of that most ubiquitous and amazing of all substances, water. Water, unlike most substances on earth, exists in all three phases—gaseous, liquid, and solid—within the tiny range of atmospheric conditions found here on earth. Due to this "versatility," clouds can suddenly appear and disappear, and "precipitate," pelting us with rain and snow. While these events are commonplace to us, in a cosmic sense, they are nothing less than miraculous. And there is still considerable mystery. . . . The sky itself, where we can most easily appreciate these miracles, can be a joy, revealing something new every day if we would but look.

I stopped there.

"If we would but look." This was an invitation.

"Look." This was an imperative. And it seemed directed at me.

I scrounged in my purse for a scrap of paper and a pen to jot down the name and address that appeared in fine print at the bottom of the poster. I'd get a cloud poster of my own. I'd learn to speak Cloud Latin. I'd read the skies and know the clouds by name. I'd make up for decades of lost time. It wasn't too late.

At long last, but too soon, my neighbor appeared, packed and ready to go. I was not. Reluctantly, I turned away from the clouds and helped my neighbor carry her bags to my car. We arrived at the station just moments before the train pulled in. I waved her off, then drove straight home—on fire over clouds. I had a lot of cloud watching in my future. But first a small mystery to solve. Who was the creative genius behind the poster?

Two weeks and several dead ends later, I had tracked down Art Rangno—the photographer, writer, and producer of the *Guide to the Sky* poster. In our first phone conversation, I learned that the poster I had seen was one of twelve editions Art had published between 1987 and 2005 during his distinguished thirty-year career in research meteorology at the University of Washington in Seattle. As a specialist in airborne studies of clouds, Art had served as the flight meteorologist or flight scientist on more than seven hundred research flights. He knew clouds inside and out, as a scientist and an admirer. In addition to writing the poetic poster captions, he had authored many articles on clouds for scientific journals over the years. I understood little of what Art told me about his research during that phone call, but I could tell without a doubt that he was crazy about clouds and eager to share his knowledge and enthusiasm. As luck would have it, Art had just retired and moved to Tucson, Arizona, and happily accepted my request to be "my meteorologist" during my pursuit of the clouds.

I did not expect to be swept off my feet by clouds, although I should have seen it coming a few years earlier, on the day I began house hunting in the Pacific Northwest. My family and I had been living in sunny, often scorching Southern California for five years. There must have been clouds overhead sometimes, but now I can recall only the thick layer of fog referred to as "June gloom," the ubiquitous crisscrossing airplane contrails, and one iridescent swirl of cloud produced by a missile launched from a nearby military base. It was time for a change. One glorious September afternoon, I flew into Seattle, rented a car, and headed south on Interstate 5 toward Olympia. Rounding a curve, I noticed a massive pile-up of white clouds billowing up from the horizon. I squeezed the steering wheel, leaned into the windshield for a bigger view, and said out loud and loudly, "I've *missed* you guys!"

This surprised me for two reasons: One, I was talking to clouds. Two, I didn't know why I'd missed them. I had never been a cloud watcher or weather buff. I didn't even know the clouds well enough to call them something other than "guys."

Three days after seeing these billowing guys, I found a home in Olympia. In early November, my husband, twelve- and fourteen-year-old sons, family dog, and I piled into the car and left Southern California. We drove north under sunny skies for one day and then in solid, drenching, rooster-tailing rain for three.

Our 1,138-mile drive, I would learn later, occurred during one of the worst Pacific Northwest storms in a decade. During November 5–7, 2006, a "Pineapple Express" storm originating north of Hawaii hit the coast from Northern California all the way to British Columbia. Although the record-breaking rains and flooding made the national news, I have no memory of the clouds that brought all that rain.

Nor do I remember the clouds that brought the other dozen Pineapple Express storms during our first months in Olympia. I was not looking at the sky but at the ground, which was wet, puddled, or flooded. My family and I spent our days under roofs—my husband at his office, our sons at school, and me unpacking boxes and shopping for rain gear and Vitamin D supplements. We tried to make the best of the weather our first winter. We took walks during brief "sun breaks." We covered our eyes as if blinded by the glare and asked, "What's that shiny yellow thing?" I referred to the rain as "liquid sunshine" until my older son told me glumly, "Mom, it's just not that funny."

Our moods sank.

Our tans faded.

The dog scowled.

The euphoria I had experienced seeing those clouds on the freeway was long gone—smothered under the persistent blankets of gray clouds that were spitting, drizzling, showering, or gushing—or threatening to. I tried to ignore them. I kept my gaze downward as I searched for a subject for my next book on natural history. I studied field guides about the Pacific Northwest, learned about moss and slugs, volunteered to survey floodplains for frog eggs, salvaged native plants from construction sites, and dug holes for a schoolyard garden. Not until two years later, during my encounter with the cloud poster, did it occur to me to look up and see what the clouds had to offer.

After returning home from the train station, my life with clouds began. When I was inside I looked out. When I was outside I looked up. I walked under tumultuous skies and settled ones, during sun breaks and showers. My perfunctory dog walks became cloud rambles—my leashed dog pulling forward while I gazed upward. I tripped on curbs. I fell over my dog. Once I walked into a parked car. The clouds were beguiling, astonishing, and entertaining—incessantly so. Day after day I saw new and different ones.

Hour by hour, minute by minute, they changed shape, color, and opacity, and how they played with the sun and landscape.

I pedaled my white fat-tire bike (which I dubbed *Cloud Chaser*) to parks and open fields around town to discover new cloud-viewing spots. I steered it through huge rain puddles when they held the reflection of parting white clouds and blue sky, and sometimes it seemed possible to bike down into the sky and onto the tops of the clouds. So realistic was this roadside trompe l'oeil that I found myself gripping my handlebars extra tightly to keep from falling up.

I hoped the clouds would reveal a pattern across the seasons, a rhythm to each day. Yet the clouds divulged nothing. They were simply beautiful and more beautiful, mysterious and ever more mysterious. The more longingly I gazed at them, the more unfathomable they became. I memorized their ten Latin names, but the ones I spotted never quite matched the ones on my *Guide to the Sky* poster. Looking at the sky became less joyful and more frustrating. On some mornings, I refused to look up, knowing the clouds would remind me of how little I had learned.

The clouds were too beautiful, too dynamic, and too enigmatic.

The clouds did not explain themselves, and so I turned to meteorology textbooks and field guides to the weather.

And this is where my trouble began.

I did not really know what a cloud was.

A Note of Caution

It took me a long time to find my way into the clouds. I lost my way frequently, and were it not for another strange encounter with a hallway and a door years before, I might have given up. Recalling this encounter provided me with a compass of sorts, one that put me at ease as I made my way.

I was on my way to a new class in a two-story office building on the corner of a busy downtown intersection. It was a yoga class, though this is irrelevant. What is pertinent is that the yoga studio occupied the front corner of the building and had big storefront windows on both sides. Big signs and banners with the studio's name doubled as privacy shades from the street. While the studio itself was obvious from the street, the entrance to the studio was not.

I parked my car nearby and walked toward what looked like the entry door. It was locked. I walked around the corner to a door on the other side of the studio. That one was locked too. I continued farther along the side of the building to an unmarked door. I pulled, and it opened. I stepped into a vestibule and looked for signs to the studio. There were none.

I walked down a dim corridor lined with closed doors of various small businesses, none offering yoga classes. At a dead end I found an elevator. I pushed the button. The elevator arrived, and I got on. There were buttons for three floors. I pushed the middle one. I stepped out into another hallway with more office doors. This hall only led to another dead end. I started giggling. I turned around and walked back toward the elevator, but instead of retracing my steps, I took the stairs as if to somehow outsmart this labyrinth. I walked down a flight of stairs, opened the door, and walked into an interior lobby facing the wide open doors to the yoga studio.

I walked toward a small desk where a woman, the teacher I presumed, sat in her yoga togs in an aura of calm.

"Hi!" I blurted out. "I'm glad I found my way in! The entrance from the street wasn't exactly obvious so I—"

I recounted my story of the locked entrance doors, the elevator, the dead-end hallways, and the stairway. She listened patiently but didn't smile or acknowledge that the entrance was a problem.

Instead she handed me a pen, gestured toward the sign-in sheet, and said matter-of-factly, "The way you do anything is the way you do everything."

CLOUD

*A **cloud** is a visible mass of water droplets or ice crystals suspended in the atmosphere above the earth.*

I recognized a cloud when I saw one, of course, but I couldn't explain what made a cloud a cloud and not something else, such as smoke, haze, steam, or mist. I knew clouds were made of water and that they floated, but so did icebergs. What kind of water were clouds made of? Was it plain old water—H_2O—or something more special? Was fog a cloud? What were the defining features of a cloud?

My beloved 1980 *Webster's New Collegiate Dictionary* lists several senses and sub-senses of the word "cloud." The sense I was interested in, an atmospheric cloud, appears at the top of the list and is defined as "a visible mass of particles of water or ice in the form of fog, mist, or haze suspended usu. at considerable height in the air."

This did little to clarify the clouds for me or to conjure up a cloud in my mind's eye. Although the definition was not stellar, the cloud chart printed next to it was exquisite. The chart was the size of a stick of chewing gum and featured ten tiny clouds rendered in pen and ink with such delicate lines that I imagined the artist used the same fine nib to write haiku on grains of rice. Each illustration captured the distinct qualities of ten different clouds—a real achievement given the enormous, soft, pale masses they depicted.

My *Webster's* etymological notes contained the best clues to the physical appearance of clouds. The word "cloud" is derived from or related to the words "rock" and "clod."

Intrigued, I hoisted the first volume of my 1971 *Oxford English Dictionary* (OED) from my bookshelf, dusted off the magnifying lens it came with, and began reading.

The word "cloud" first appeared around the end of the thirteenth century and is derived from the Old English *clûd*, meaning a mass of stone, rock, boulder, hill, or other earthen form. *Clûd* is related to "clod," a word we know and use (though rarely) to describe a lump of dirt. In the agrarian society of the thirteenth century, however, clods were common (as dirt) and perhaps best known by the clodhoppers, whose job it was to walk behind the horse-drawn plow and stomp on the unbroken clods to prepare a field for planting. The OED notes that "cloud" was first used to describe clouds later known as Cumulus—the clumpy, clod-like ones.

This left me wondering if early speakers of English had other names (now lost) for wispy and layered clouds or whether they didn't speak about these clouds.

According to the OED, the word "cloud" appears in other languages in recognizable variations to describe clod-shaped things: Dutch *kluit* ("lump, mass, clod"), German/Low German *Kluut/Kluute* ("lump, mass, ball"), German *Kloß* ("lump, dumpling, meatball"), Danish *klode* ("sphere, orb, planet"), Swedish *klot* ("sphere, orb, ball, globe"), and Icelandic *klót* ("knob on a sword's hilt").

My dictionaries indicate that "cloud" is also akin to *gloutos* or "glute." Really? As in glutes, *gluteus maximus*, the butt muscles? Exactly. *Gloutos*, the Greek word for buttocks, was borrowed to describe clouds before the words sounding like "clod" were introduced. I could hear the similarities in "glute" and "clod" (especially when I said them out loud) and could see the buttocks shape in certain rounded Cumulus clouds. Greek speakers, however, do not refer to clouds as glutes.

The Greek word for cloud is *nephos* or *nephele*. In Greek mythology, Nephele is the name of a cloud nymph and also the goddess of hospitality. We find "neph" at the root of archaic or rarely used words such as "nephology" (the study of clouds—not to be confused with "nephrology," the study of kidneys), "nephologist" (a specialist in the study of clouds), "nepheligenous" (emitting clouds, especially tobacco smoke), and "nepheliad" (a cloud nymph).

Unable to put the magnifying glass down, I found my way to "nep," a term the OED informs me was used in the United States in the nineteenth century to describe a "small lump or knot in imperfect cotton-fibers." More lumps!

In many Romance languages, words for "cloud" are derived from the Latin *nubes*, meaning cloud. From this we have *nubes* in Spanish, *nube*, *nuvolo*, and *nuvola* in Italian, *nuvem* in Portuguese, *nubo* in Esperanto, and then *nuage* in French. In English "nub" means knob or lump, from which come words such as nebula (a cloud of stars), nebulize (to reduce to a fine spray or mist), nebulous (indistinct, vague), obnubilate (to make unclear or cloudy), nebulaphobia (fear of clouds), and nuance (shade, as in shade of meaning). The roots of clouds were deeper and more widespread than I imagined.

From the letter N, it wasn't far to M and "meteorology," the branch of science that includes the study of the atmosphere, weather, and clouds. The word "meteor" is a combination of two Greek words—*meta* (with, among) and *eoroes* (related to air and to lift). The World Meteorological Organization, an agency of the United Nations, defines a meteor as a "phenomenon observed in the atmosphere or on the surface of the Earth." The flashes and streaks of light associated with asteroids, comets, meteorites, and "shooting stars" represent but one type of meteor, the lithometeor. Rainbows and other optical phenomena produced by sunlight or moonlight are known as photometeors. Manifestations of atmospheric electricity, such as lightning, thunder, and polar auroras, are classified as electrometeors. And clouds, all forms of precipitation, dew, waterspouts, and tornadoes are all hydrometeors.

Despite these classifications, common usage seems to rule. No one I know refers to clouds or raindrops as meteors. No one would think to bring an umbrella to a meteor shower. Meteors are shooting stars, rain is rain, clouds are clouds.

Returning now to *Webster's*, I read its definition of "cloud" again: "a visible mass of particles of water or ice in the form of fog, mist, or haze suspended usu. at considerable height in the air."

Something was wrong.

And it wasn't the odd abbreviation of "usu." for "usually." The definition was vague—nebulous, if you will. What was the difference between fog, mist, and haze? What was considered a "considerable" height? Were clouds *in* the air or did they float *on* the air?

Hoping for more clarity, I consulted a few more up-to-date weather books, meteorology textbooks, and online dictionaries. Some definitions of "cloud" were clearer, others more muddled.

I was faced with a dilemma: I could pretend that I understood the gist of a cloud and move on, or I could be obtuse.

I chose the latter.

From twelve different sources, I copied out twelve different definitions of "cloud." I marked the words that appeared in at least three of the definitions. Ten key words emerged: visible, mass, water, droplets, ice, crystals, suspended, atmosphere, above, earth. By adding a few prepositions and articles, I created a new definition: "A cloud is a visible mass of water droplets or ice crystals suspended in the atmosphere above the earth."

I read the definition again and again, each time more slowly than the next, lingering on each word. My definition was accurate and lean. Each word had a quintessential purity and pleasing heft. Memorizing my definition and reciting it like a mantra led to a major "aha!" moment: I did not understand what a cloud was, nor did I understand the meaning of the words that defined one. What actually made something visible? Were there invisible clouds? How big is a mass? Are water droplets different from raindrops? Are ice crystals all shaped like snowflakes? How does a cloud get suspended? Where exactly is the atmosphere? What's in the atmosphere that makes clouds possible?

In the face of so many big questions, I was tempted to give up on clouds. They seemed unreachable and unknowable. I read my definition again and again. Each word felt like a stepping-stone—no, more like a door. A door I could open. A door I could wander through to find my way into the clouds.

The Danger Zone

In search of the cloud-savvy people in my community, I signed up for a SkyWarn Weather Spotter training class. The class was being offered in a neighboring county by the National Weather Service and the National Oceanic and Atmospheric Administration (NOAA), which have trained thousands of volunteers across the country to recognize and report the early warning signs of severe weather. It was reassuring to know that our federal government valued what people like me might be able to tell them about clouds. And it felt good to know that I might be able to help our local emergency response teams mitigate against disasters caused by storms, flooding, tornadoes, high winds, and blizzards.

With Olympia's "mild maritime" climate, I figured the two-hour training would be light on "severe" weather and heavy on cloud identification. It would be a triple win for me: I'd learn about my local clouds, tap into the cloud-loving subculture, and turn my idle cloud watching into public good.

Thirty-five of us future SkyWarn Weather Spotters gathered one evening in a classroom at the Mason County Emergency Management building north of Olympia. There were equal numbers of men and women, most older than me. All were in flannel or fleece, none in an "I ♡ clouds" sweatshirt.

Our two instructors were quick to address our "mild" climate and nip in the bud any complacency we might have about our responsibilities. There have been more presidentially declared weather-related disasters in Washington since 1950 than in any other state, they informed us. Windstorms, snowstorms, heavy rain, widespread and major flooding, wildfires, and tornado strikes occur with alarming frequency here. We were not expected to take their word for it, however. They brought backup evidence.

The video began with a time-lapse sequence of benign white clouds churning along to an energetic, upbeat soundtrack of Baroque violin. Within seconds, however, the music turned sour, the clouds grew dark and menacing, and the pummeling began.

Mudflows gushed down roadways like raging rivers, culverts collapsed into flooded streams, traffic lights swung wildly in hurricane-force winds, snow blew sideways into stranded cars, mobile homes lay shattered and strewn, barns and farmland disappeared under floodwaters. This was my state? My mild, maritime climate?

Aghast, I watched. And listened. The soundtrack of the video montage also featured wailing electric guitars and an amped-up Kenny Loggins singing "Danger Zone," the testosterone-and-jet-fueled theme song of the movie *Top Gun*.

"Highway to the danger zone. Gonna take you to the . . . danger zone! Right into the danger zone." Over and over and over.

I felt so sorry for the clouds.

It occurred to me that damage wrought by severe weather is caused by wind, snow, ice, rain, hail, and lightning—not by the clouds themselves. We malign clouds as harbingers of bad weather and agents of destruction, but they are either benign or beneficial most of the time.

The PowerPoint presentation that followed further demonized the clouds. Amid images of blizzards, blowing volcanic ash, lightning, and baseball-sized hailstones were funnel-shaped tornado clouds and the dark clouds, wall clouds, and shelf clouds associated with them. And there was fog—dense, ship-wrecking, car-crashing fog.

Now I felt peeved and defensive on the clouds' behalf. What about the Cumulus, the Cirrus, the Altocumulus perlucidus, and the many other lovely, harmless clouds I had seen in the cloud poster? Nothing.

Now it was quiz time.

The instructors projected an image of a "severe-weather" cloud from the presentation and asked us to identify it. They tossed chocolate candies to the first student who called out the correct answer. I didn't even try. I sat with my arms crossed, as if this would send a clear message to the instructors—and therefore to the staffs of the National Weather Service and NOAA—that their treatment of the clouds was unfair and unjust. I don't think the instructors noticed.

At the end of the class, I received my complementary rain gauge, a sixteen-by-sixteen-inch white board for collecting snow in our yard, and a twenty-inch metal gauge for measuring the snow that fell on the board to the tenth of an inch.

By the time my course-completion certificate arrived in the mail a few weeks later, I had decided that I did not want to measure the rain or snow. I wasn't motivated to watch for clouds that spelled danger. Watching for troublesome clouds was akin to keeping an eye on a roomful of kindergarteners just to spot the one kid about to haul off and punch a classmate. As a SkyWarn Weather Spotter, I wouldn't be really looking at clouds, I'd just be looking for trouble.

Cloudy All Day

According to the National Weather Service, "cloudy" means that 7/8 or more of the sky is covered by clouds. By this definition, Olympia is cloudy 228 days a year. Add in "mostly cloudy" (5/8–7/8 cloud cover) and "partly cloudy" (3/8–5/8 cloud cover) days and suddenly almost every day is some kind of cloudy. I assumed that people living in such a cloudy city would talk about clouds the way they talked about the tides, salmon runs, and the Seahawks—often and sometimes incessantly. Yet no one I talked with or accidentally eavesdropped on ever mentioned the clouds—not by a specific Latin name, nickname, or even generically as "clouds." Locals complained about the rainy weather, but they did not talk about clouds.

So I began asking around. During a lull in a conversation, I'd drop in a casual, "So, do you know anything about clouds?"

"You mean their names and all that? Squat."

"I used to know what they were called."

"There are the ones that look like flying saucers, but I can't remember what they're called."

"Hmmm. I know I like the pink ones!"

"Clouds? We only got one type around here."

One of the very few conversations I had about clouds, however brief, occurred at a local brewpub. One late-winter night I met up with a friend, a Seattle native, who had recently returned to the area after a decade in Southern California. After we ordered our beers and settled in near the fireplace, I asked her how she was doing.

She sighed deeply and said, "Depressed. There's just gray and nothing else."

"It hasn't been all gray," I contradicted. "The clouds have been amazing!"

"Yeah," she snorted. "*Clouds*. That means *cloudy*. It sucks."

In other words, clouds are to blame for the gloomy weather and gloomy moods of those who live under them, even though the skies on many "partly cloudy" days might be mostly blue. But this is not what comes to mind when we think "cloudy." We think of low layers of gray clouds and rain. This is unfortunate but understandable. Our rainy season in the temperate Pacific Northwest lasts from October through March—the time of year when the sun rises late, barely clears the tops of the trees as it arcs across the southern sky, and then sets early. Our northern latitude (Olympia sits at 47.04° N) is partly to blame, but the rain is too. According to the National Weather Service, this is the time of year Olympia gets most of its 50 inches. But this isn't all that much rain. Miami gets more—57.1 inches annually—but no one describes Miami as cloudy; it is cloudy only 115 days a year.

Miami is sunnier but rainier than Olympia.

Olympia is cloudier but drier than Miami.

Cloudy does not mean rainy.

Cloudy does not necessarily mean gloomy.

Most importantly, cloudy does not suck.

I was puzzled by the lack of knowledge about the clouds in Olympia, a city where locals shun umbrellas and invest heavily in outdoor gear, waterproof clothing, rubber-soled shoes, and all-weather hairstyles. I had a hunch there were cloud-savvy boaters, mountaineers, and airplane pilots around town, but I was more interested in what nonspecialists knew—the people whose lives or livelihoods did not depend on an awareness or knowledge of clouds, the people who unwittingly ignored them, the people who had forgotten everything they might have learned about them. My people!

I also had a hunch that "my people" were not only in Olympia but also elsewhere across the country. To find them, I created an online survey and invited friends, family, and acquaintances to answer ten friendly questions about clouds. In a few weeks, sixty-seven people responded. My survey was anonymous, although I knew I had reached a mix of men and women, kindergarteners through octogenarians, professional scientists, science fiction fans, those with window offices and those without, East Coasters and West Coasters, outdoorsy types, indoorsy types, boaters, and at least one backyard clothesline user who watched the skies for rain. The results were informative, fascinating, and often hilarious.

Cloud Survey Question

 How many clouds can you name? Please list.

> *altus*
> *cumonubis*
> *cutaneous*
> *cirius*
> *circus*
> *columnar*
> *the bushy ones—cumulus—right?*
> *how the hell do you spell cumulus/cumulous?*
> *the fifth one (nebulus ones??)*
> *nebulous*
> *something starting with the letter "N" (nimbus???)*
> *nimbus*

thunder

stratosomething

venticular

do airplane contrails count?

clouds that look like sharks, care bears, and tufted upholstery

rain clouds

fluffy ones

long stringy ones

wispy and foreboding

horse tails

crap, okay, so I don't know many clouds

In addition to creative replies such as these, respondents listed correctly as many as eight of the ten most common official Latin cloud names, with most falling in the two-to-three range. Before I started watching the clouds, my answers would have fallen in the low range too: only mare's tails, thunderheads, and Cumulus. What makes these Latin names so hard to remember? Have a look at them:

Cirrus

Cirrostratus

Cirrocumulus

Altocumulus

Altostratus

Nimbostratus

Cumulonimbus

Cumulus

Stratocumulus

Stratus

The ten names are all made up of only twelve letters: A, I, O, U, B, C, L, M, N, R, S, and T. And they are based on just five Latin terms (*cirrus, cumulus, stratus, alto, nimbus*), which appear alone or coupled with nearly identical modifiers ("cirro," "cumulo," "strato," "alto," and "nimbo") and always end with "us." The logic behind their coupling is neither intuitive nor explained in any book I read. Why, for instance, is it Cumulonimbus and not Nimbocumulus? Why Stratocumulus and not Cumulostratus? Why is Nimbostratus the only cloud with a unique beginning, nimbo? Why use "alto"—which actually means high—to describe mid-level clouds (Altocumulus and Altostratus)?

You might think that learning the meaning of the five Latin terms would make the cloud names easier to learn: *stratus* = layer, *cumulus* = heap, *cirrus* = wisps, *alto* = high (mid-level, in cloudspeak), *nimbus* = rain. Yet even with these translations, I struggled to combine them correctly to create a legitimate cloud name, much less use them to describe an actual cloud.

Who stuck us with these ten names? Whose dubious achievement was this nomenclatural nightmare?

A Checker'd History

It was not a failed Latin student or a ne'er-do-well scientist who developed our current cloud-naming system. It was thirty-three-year-old Luke Howard, a well-respected English chemist with a lifelong love of clouds.

Howard presented his Latin cloud names in a lecture he gave to fellow scientists in London in 1802. His lecture was enthusiastically received, according to Richard Hamblyn's marvelous book *The Invention of Clouds: How an Amateur Meteorologist Forged the Language of the Skies*. Hamblyn writes that Luke Howard's audience considered his ideas "elegant," "so clear and so self-evident," his language "sublime."

Howard's audience of fifty may have been wowed, but I was not. At least not until I learned about some of the zanier cloud-naming schemes that came before his.

Philosopher-naturalists from Thales of Miletus in the sixth century BC and Aristotle in the fourth century BC to Descartes in the seventeenth century AD had published relatively sophisticated theories on the physical properties and formation of clouds, but none had developed names for them. It was not until 1655 that the first real attempt was made to order the chaos of the skies. In that year, Robert Hooke, the English physicist and founding member of the Royal Society of London, began an ambitious project to create "A Method for Making a History of the Weather." He enlisted volunteers to keep daily records of the weather and appearance of the sky. They recorded temperature, humidity, and the speed and direction of the wind using numbers and special symbols, but they used words—often many of them—to describe the sky and clouds. "Clear blew but yellowish in the N.E. Clowded toward the S. Checker'd blew." "Sunset red and hazy." "Overcast and very lowring &c."

Eventually, Hooke pared down their unwieldy descriptions to nine single words:

Cleer
Checker'd
Hazy
Thick
Hairy
Water'd
Waved
Cloudy
Lowring

A bit quaint, I'd say. But Richard Hamblyn says this was a "huge step forward": Hooke's list represents the "first true attempt in Western science to mould a descriptive vocabulary to fit the fleeting appearances of the sky."

Hooke certainly deserves credit for his "descriptive vocabulary," but only four of his nine names—"thick," "hairy," "waved," and "low'ring"—described clouds. Only the "hairy" sky described a specific cloud we would recognize today: cirrus. Most of Hooke's names—"cleer," "checker'd," "hazy," "watered," and "cloudy"—described the skies. Hooke's explanation of these terms did little to help a cloud watcher identify or name specific clouds. He described a "cloudy" sky, for example, as one that "has many thick dark Clouds" and a "checker'd" sky as one featuring "many great white round Clouds, such as are very usual in summer."

Had Hooke refined his cloud names and introduced a system for using them—one reflecting the dynamic nature of clouds—he might have been credited with forging the language of the skies. But, according to Hamblyn's research, this virtuosic scientist "hurried from one inquiry to another with brilliant but inconclusive results." Within months of publishing his description of the sky in 1665, the thirty-year-old Hooke abandoned the clouds to study fossils, diving bells, pendulums, human memory, and other subjects that piqued his interest.

Another cloud-classification system did not emerge for 115 years, when a meteorological society was established in 1780 to study long-range weather patterns and to predict changes in the weather. The Palatine Meteorological Society, headquartered in Mannheim, Germany, operated a network of weather stations across Europe and the Northern Hemisphere. For more than

a decade, personnel at each station recorded all kinds of data, including the types of clouds they observed. They assigned twelve names to the clouds:
White
Grey
Dark
Orange-yellow
Red
Thin
Thick
Streak-like
Rock-like
Disc-shaped
Layered
Gathering

While still far from the Latin cloud names we use today, these adjectives did describe the clouds and not the sky around them. While the color names could be applied to many clouds, the other names seem to describe specific cloud forms we would recognize today. "Rock-like" struck me as an apt term for Cumulus and "Layered" apt for Stratus, Nimbostratus, and Altostratus.

Though the society's cloud names struck me as being as static as Hooke's, the real contribution of the society wasn't the names per se but the use of them in combination. A cloud could be white *and* rock-like. It could be white and rock-like and gathering. It could be dark and gathering. Clouds were allowed to be complex and changeable in a way they had not been considered before. This bold solution, Hamblyn believes, might have endured had the society not disbanded when the city of Mannheim was destroyed in 1795 during turmoil of war across Europe.

Next on the cloud front was Jean-Baptiste-Pierre-Antoine de Monet de Lamarck—a man whose name suggests he was well suited to nomenclatural challenges. Lamarck (as he is usually known, thank goodness) was a celebrated biologist, philosopher, evolutionary theorist, and curator of the national museum of natural history in Paris. Lamarck and other scientists of his day worked under the influence of Carl von Linné (Carolus Linnaeus), who in 1735 had introduced his binomial system for naming living things and had developed a system for classifying these living things by their perceived similarities or differences in form. Lamarck observed that clouds too tended to appear in a limited number of basic forms. This revolutionarily simple insight did not lead Lamarck to develop a simple Linnean system for naming these basic forms. In 1802, Lamarck began publishing his first of many sets of names for broad groups of clouds. Using the French word *nuages* for clouds, he gave us *nuages en forme de voile* (clouds in the form of a veil), *nuages attroupes* (massed), *nuages pommeles* (dappled), *nuages en balayeurs* (broomlike, swept), *nuages groupes* (grouped), and *nuages en lambeaux* (torn clouds).

According to Richard Hamblyn, Lamarck's terms described neither general forms nor specific clouds but "secondary characteristics of shape, colour, and texture." Lamarck was merely naming the clouds, not classifying them, and he was doing so in French despite the fact that Latin was gaining popularity as the international language of science. Although Lamarck's vague and peculiar French names didn't endure, his idea that clouds should be grouped by altitude did. Clouds, he observed, occurred mostly in one of three *étages*, or levels, which he named low, middle, and high. That different clouds tend to occur at different altitudes might seem obvious to us today, but prior to the first piloted hot-air balloons in the late 1700s, the height of clouds could not be accurately measured or truly appreciated.

Though Howard and Lamarck had never met and were not in any apparent competition with each other to name the clouds, Luke Howard presented his paper on cloud types in 1802, the very year Lamarck began publishing his names. But Howard succeeded where Lamarck failed, partly because he imitated the increasingly popular Linnaean binomial system for naming plants and animals. Howard introduced seven cloud types: three basic forms (Cumulus, Cirrus, and Stratus) and four variations (Cirro-cumulus, Cirro-stratus, Cumulo-stratus, and Cirro-cumulo-stratus). Howard called each of these variations "modifications" because he believed the clouds existed on a continuum, with each cloud being essentially a modification of another cloud.

Finally, after centuries of vague, quaint, and provincial cloud names, the world had a manageable set of names within an accepted scientific framework. It must have been a relief to both Luke Howard and the scientific community to have finally devised a way to pin down the ephemeral, changeable clouds.

Howard's cloud names were published in 1803, with the addition of "Nimbus" to indicate clouds that rained. In 1817, he reorganized his list to order the clouds by altitude, as had Lamarck. Over the next several decades, meteorologists regularly modified Howard's cloud names and adopted the Linnaean classification scheme to turn Howard's "modifications" into "genera" (the plural of genus). The International Meteorological Organization, established in 1877, assumed the role of standardizing the names and descriptions of the clouds and in 1896 published the first edition of the *International Cloud Atlas*. With but one exception—the change of Nimbus to Nimbostratus in 1930—this first atlas includes the names of the ten cloud genera we use today as well as general height classifications.

Subsequent editions of the atlas were produced by the International Meteorological Organization, which in 1951 became the World Meteorological Organization. The atlas is the standard reference document for professional cloud observers, and it is widely used for weather forecasting and longer-term climate prediction by meteorologists, those working in aviation and at sea, and amateur cloud watchers.

When I began my study of clouds, the *International Cloud Atlas* was in two volumes: one last updated in 1975, the other in 1987. The books were long out of print, and so I visited university libraries to read reference copies of this authoritative work myself. It features information on the ten cloud forms— Cirrus, Cirrostratus, Cirrocumulus, Altocumulus, Altostratus, Nimbostratus, Cumulonimbus, Cumulus, Stratocumulus, and Stratus. These basic forms, which evolved from Luke Howard's list, are officially referred to as "genera."

Just as Linnaeus subdivided each plant and animal genera into species, so has the World Meteorological Organization subdivided each cloud genus. Unlike a living species, which you may recall is defined by its ability to reproduce fertile offspring, clouds do not reproduce or have sex (though they do seem to multiply in the sky). A cloud species is instead defined by its characteristic shape or internal structure.

There are fifteen different cloud species, each with a Latin name. For instance, in the genus Stratus, there are two species: "fractus" refers to a Stratus with a ragged, shredded appearance; "nebulosus" refers to one with a featureless, layered look. Each cloud genus can be accompanied by only one species name, with the exception of Nimbostratus and Altostratus—two clouds considered so uniform in shape and structure that they are not classified into species.

In addition to the ten genera and fifteen species, clouds are further subdivided into nine categories known as varieties. Plants are also classified as "varieties" and animals as the equivalent "subspecies." Cloud varieties are grouped by their degrees of transparency and arrangement of their elements—the smaller clumps and wisps that make up a larger cloud formation. If, for instance, the layers of a Stratus nebulosus appear to undulate, that cloud can be called a Stratus nebulosus undulatus.

The clouds have not made it easy for us to talk about them.

As I researched the history of cloud names, I let my meteorologist know of my efforts to learn all the official Latin names of the clouds. His response was less enthusiastic than I hoped.

"I admire your persistence," he wrote, "but frankly the ID-ing of clouds has become a bit passé."

Passé?

He told me that the newest edition of a popular meteorology textbook had "dropped the section in which they discussed cloud forms. I think it seems archaic now."

Archaic?

Ouch.

Apparently, professional meteorologists don't need to identify more than the basic ten cloud types for official reporting procedures and weather forecasting. Most of the Latin species and variety names I was trying to memorize were introduced in the 1939 and 1956 editions of the *International Cloud Atlas* to help observers make distinctions between similar clouds and to facilitate an understanding of the evolution and transformation of these clouds. These names preceded the invention and widespread use of Doppler radar, LIDAR, weather satellites, and other technologies that now provide meteorologists with more accurate and complete information about the clouds and the atmosphere than the cloud names could. In fact, meteorology students at many colleges are now required only to differentiate clouds composed of liquid water droplets from clouds composed of ice crystals, features that provide a snapshot of the temperature and humidity of the local atmosphere.

Relying on "droplet" and "crystal" would have greatly simplified my study of the clouds, but I wasn't ready to abandon learning Cloud Latin, especially after I learned that the World Meteorological Organization planned to publish a new edition of the *International Cloud Atlas* as a web-based digital publication, which they did in March 2017. The new atlas includes eleven newly named cloud features as well as hundreds of high-resolution photographs of clouds documented with metadata. The digital age has ushered in a new generation of enthusiastic cloud watchers with smartphone cameras handy, thumbs poised to share photos and—with a little push—send Latin cloud names flying around the globe.

I am thrilled about the new atlas for many reasons, but mostly for reviving a language that might easily have become "archaic" and "passé" without a new generation of users. It is human nature to name things, to use language to make sense of the world around us. These names are what we most often want to know first about a cloud we see: "What's that one called?" The names allow us to talk about clouds. Stating this seems obvious, but not knowing the clouds' names for most of my life had, in effect, kept me from talking about them. Not talking about something makes that something easier to ignore. I needed to look at the clouds. I needed to talk about the clouds.

How to Talk about Clouds

The Latin names, unfortunately, make a lousy introduction to clouds. The names are overwhelming, confusing, a put-off. When I began watching the clouds, the Latin names left me nearly speechless and reminded me of my oldest son when he was about six months old. He would slap his hand down on a big pillow and say one word, "dat." Then he'd slap his hand down on the blanket and say it again: "dat." Then the book I was reading him, "dat." A smaller pillow, "dat." Everything was different, but everything was "dat." Eventually the difference between objects—a big pillow and a little pillow, this book and that book, for example—made sense to him, and his vocabulary grew to reflect his knowledge.

With little knowledge of the clouds around me, I found it easy to avoid using the Latin names. I could just point to a particular cloud and call it a cloud ("dat"). Once I really started looking at them, however, I realized I could distinguish this cloud from that cloud and then low from high, puffy from layered, and clumpy from wispy clouds. Eventually I caught on to

Stratus, Cumulus, Cirrus, and the rest of the big ten but didn't feel the desire to take on the species and variety names until much later—after I met a cloud with five names.

This particular cloud appeared in a swath of the eastern sky while I was driving in downtown Olympia one day. I pulled over and got out of my car to get a better look. Dozens of little clouds—white, oval ones—radiated in orderly rows and columns from a point on the horizon. I had never seen such clouds in the sky or in a photograph. They looked artificial, as if someone had projected an image of flattened marshmallows onto the blue sky as an urban art installation.

I couldn't linger, so I took some photographs and drove on. That evening, I tried to find my cloud in one of my field guides. There weren't any remotely like mine. Excited that I had perhaps captured a never-before-seen cloud, I found my way to the website of the Cloud Appreciation Society, a London-based organization for cloud lovers worldwide. I posted my photo on the discussion forum with a query: "What kind of clouds are these?" My grammar was wrong (it is either "kind of cloud" or "kinds of clouds"), but I wasn't sure if my photograph showed a single complex cloud or many closely spaced individual clouds.

A reply came by the next morning from someone posting as "H."

"I would think Altocumulus stratiformis perlucidus undulatus radiatus."

Surely, "H" was pulling my leg. But, no, this was a legitimate designation in the cloud lexicon—one genus name (Altocumulus), one species (stratiformis), and three variety names. Though this particular cloud was not named in the *International Cloud Atlas*, "H" had studied my photograph and skillfully applied all the names that suited my cloud. This, apparently, is how the language of the clouds works; speakers select names from a list and combine them to the best of their abilities. Someone posting as "M" might have changed the order of the variety names or even added another variety name to the five "H" provided. As long as variety names are added in the order of predominance of the particular feature (as judged by the observer), the cloud name is grammatically correct.

So why give a cloud five names when "some type of Altocumulus" would suffice? To be more precise. Because you can be. Or at least "H" could. And I wanted to too. Perhaps knowing the clouds' full names would help me get to know them better.

Altocumulus stratiformis perlucidus undulatus radiatus cloud

What did the five names tell me about such a cloud? "Alto" means that the cloud's base occurs at mid-level, between 6,500 and 23,000 feet above the earth. My cloud was heaped (*cumulus*), and because these heaps appeared as extensive sheets or layers (*strati*) in form (*formis*), my cloud was an Altocumulus stratiformis. Because the layer was not uniformly solid but composed of individual cloudlets separated by gaps showing blue sky, my cloud was Altocumulus stratiformis perlucidus (*perlucidus* relating to "perlucid," an obsolete variation of "pellucid," meaning "to allow the passage of light"). Because of its undulating pattern, it took on a fourth name--undulatus. And a fifth--radiatuas--because it appeared to radiate from one point on the horizon.

Altocumulus stratiformis perlucidus undulatus radiatus.

Twenty-one syllables.

Five names.

Many cloudlets.

One cloud formation.

One cloud I will never forget.

Identifying and naming a cloud an Altocumulus stratiformis perlucidus undulatus radiatus means you have studied the cloud carefully, as "H" obviously had. When "H" attached this name to my photograph, it helped me to see and appreciate each of the five characteristics of this cloud. Had I posted a video clip of this cloud, perhaps "H" would have added a few more names to describe the evolution or transformation of the cloud. Had someone less observant or less fluent in Cloud Latin responded to my query, my cloud might have a shorter name. Both long and short names are considered correct, the longer name just more complete. Fluency in cloud names is less about showing off than showing attention, even love, for these natural wonders.

Through language, strange and nameless clouds can be recognized, discussed, and understood. Through language, once-distant relationships to clouds can become familiar, intimate, enduring.

As with clouds, there is a special kind of intimacy in knowing the middle names of friends and family members. These names hold stories of honored namesakes, family lineage, and our younger parents' (sometimes embarrassing) notions of tradition or whimsy. Middle names aren't exactly private, but among new friends they are asked about and revealed with a bit of trepidation and only after a certain level of trust has been reached. Be alert, and you will sense the moment you're ready for a middle name. Take advantage of the moment. Your friends and the clouds will appreciate your interest.

Take it slowly at first. Don't worry about learning the species and varieties of clouds. Just start with the ten genus names then add on of the species names listed here, each with a short translation and, in parentheses, my mnemonic to make them easier for you to learn:

calvus = bald. (This describes a smooth top of a cloud. I can only think of John Calvin as a bald man to remember this one.)

capillatus = hairlike. (Perhaps you have eaten the skinny pasta called capellini or tucked your hair under your cap?)

castellanus = castle-like. (With turrets or towers and a flat base.)

congestus = gathered together. (Congested like when you have a head cold.)

fibratus = fiber-like. (Imagine a cloud made of long, stringy fibers.)

floccus = tufted. (I think of wool tufts in a flock of sheep, ragged on all sides.)

fractus = broken. (Like a fraction, fractured.)

humilis = humble. (Not a proud cloud but a low-topped one that is wider than it is tall.)

lenticularis = lentil- or lens-shaped—flat, smooth, and slightly curved on top. (Think of a lentil.)

mediocris = mediocre. ("Mediocre" is not used pejoratively here but to describe a cloud as wide as it is tall.)

nebulosus = indistinct, vague, featureless. (Think of a nebula in interstellar space. Or a nebulizer in your bathroom cabinet.)

spissatus = thickened. (This one conjures up no cognate for me, though my husband remembers that he studied inspissated—thickened—underground oil as a geology student.)

stratiformis = layered. (I think of "strata" and "stratify.")

uncinus = hooked. Pronounced *un*-sin-us. (I failed on a mnemonic here but did notice that all but one letter in this word is hook-shaped: *u n c s*.)

volutus = rolled. (Sharing the same root as "revolve," meaning to turn over and over.)

Try to apply one of the names to a cloud every once in a while. Don't be afraid of making mistakes. Only a fool or a boor would open a field guide or an app to disagree. Next, add just one of the species names to your cloud. Remember: do not add a species name to Nimbostratus or Altostratus.

Now add one or more variety names to your genus and species. You can add as many as you like ("H" used three). While your cloud might display many characteristics, make sure the names don't contradict each other. A cloud cannot be both translucent (translucidus) and opaque (opacus), for instance. The nine variety names can be added in any order.

duplicatus = in two duplicate layers.

intortus = irregular, tangled. (I think of "contorted.")

lacunosus = having gaps, spaces, missing parts. (A lacuna is a gap or space. This cloud has holes in it; it *lacks* parts.)

opacus = opaque. (Thick enough to obscure the position of the sun or moon).

perlucidus = *per* (through) + *lucid* (light). (There are gaps between the clouds, letting light shine through.)

radiatus = radiating from a center point like rays or spokes. (This is usually due to perspective; the lines are actually parallel.)

translucidus = translucent. (Thin enough to reveal the position of the sun or moon.)

undulatus = undulating. (Think of ocean waves.)

vertebratus = like spinal vertebrae. (Clouds with this name truly look like an X-ray of a spine.)

As if these descriptive terms are not enough to help you get a handle on the clouds, the World Meteorological Organization (WMO) has additional categories of accessory clouds, supplementary features, special clouds, and "mother-clouds"—and Latin names to describe them all. Supplementary features and accessory clouds occur above or below a larger cloud mass, either accompanying the cloud or attached to it. The breast-like bulges on the underside of a Cumulonimbus cloud are known as *mamma* (Latin for "breast"), and so you can call this cloud Cumulonimbus mammatus.

One of the newest supplementary features to be named is "asperitas," a chaotic, wavelike feature that occurs on the underside of clouds, mostly Altocumulus or Stratocumulus. This cloud feature was first brought to the world's attention in 2006, after a woman in Cedar Rapids, Iowa, sent a photograph she had taken of them to the Cloud Appreciation Society. It soon became clear to the society that none of the current cloud names were applicable and that the WMO should add this to its taxonomy. From their members around the world, the Cloud Appreciation Society gathered photographic evidence of clouds showing this feature and provided scientific justification to the WMO for adding this new name. The WMO accepted the new classification in 2015. Though the Cloud Appreciation Society had lobbied for a new variety named "undulatus asperatus" (undulating, roughened), the WMO and its Latin scholars decided on "asperitas" (roughness) as a supplementary feature.

Clouds that form or grow from other clouds are known as "mother-clouds." Two of my favorite new mother-cloud names are "silvagenitus" and "flammagenitus." In the case of a Stratus fractus silvagenitus, for instance, this Stratus fractus developed above a forest (silva) from moisture emitted from the trees as part of evapotranspiration. And, should that forest be consumed in a wildfire, the Cumulus congestus clouds that grew from the smoke would be known as Cumulus congestus flammagenitus.

Because the Latin names can become unwieldy, meteorologists often use a much simpler system. The National Weather Service, for instance, uses alphanumerical codes to describe the clouds in their hourly weather-data postings. Two of the ten cloud genera have their own codes: CB for Cumulonimbus and TCU for Towering Cumulus (an unofficial but common name for Cumulus congestus). The rest of the clouds are described as BKN, SCT, FEW, and OVC—"broken," "scattered," "few," and "overcast." Admittedly, using "BKN" makes more sense than a long string of Latin if you want to communicate data efficiently (from control tower to plane pilot, for instance). But speaking as an amateur cloud watcher, these words made me feel sad.

Broken.

Scattered.

Overcast.

Few.

Such words were better suited for describing the sky's flaws and short-comings than the whole, uplifting, abundant, and sometimes happy-seeming clouds. To appreciate the complexity of the clouds themselves, use the Latin names. Please. This is not about showing off or being erudite. This is about noticing what you are seeing.

Once I understood the value of the Latin names, I set out to find a complete list of Latin names for all the clouds. I figured the WMO would have calculated all the possible combinations by now. There was no list to be found in the *International Cloud Atlas*, just a chart showing columns of names to choose from to create your own combinations. The only estimate I could find for the number of named clouds was "about 100."

Sensing that this estimate was low, I asked my college-aged son if he knew of "an equation or something" that would help me calculate the specific number of known cloud classifications.

"Let me get my calculator," he said.

We sat down at the kitchen table to work. I gave him my three numbers—ten, fifteen, and nine—the numbers of the genera, species, and varieties, respectively. I showed him a list of all the names and described the rules on which species and varieties could be used with which genera. His brow furrowed.

I suggested he might need to use some symbols that meant "if this, not this" and "if this, also this, but not this."

"For instance," I said, "Stratus clouds come in two species and three varieties. The species are 'nebulosus' and 'fractus.' The varieties are 'opacus,' 'translucidus,' and 'undulatus.' According to the rules, you can have 'Stratus opacus' and 'Stratus translucidus' but not 'Stratus opacus translucidus.'"

"*Whaaat?*"

"Basically, certain modifiers exclude other modifiers. A Stratus cloud can't both hide the sun's position and also not hide it."

"You mean you can't have a cloudy cloud that's not cloudy?"

"Exactly. Can you help me?"

He studied the chart of clouds. He looked at his calculator.

He said he would need to get back to me.

It has been three years.

He has not gotten back to me.

I planned to do the math myself using the enormous whiteboard installed in my garage. As of press time, I have not gotten back to me.

How High Is That Cloud?

Most all of the clouds we see occur in the lowest layer of our atmosphere, known as the troposphere. This layer extends from the earth's surface to between 5 and 11 miles above it and is generally lower toward the poles and higher toward the equator. Within the troposphere, different clouds tend to appear within certain altitude ranges.

Recall that altitude is the height of an object above the earth and elevation is the height of landforms above sea level. Clouds float above the earth, so their height is a measurement of altitude. This may seem obvious, but I often catch myself describing the steepness of a hiking trail in terms of its altitude gain. Now that would be some hike!

Talking about the "height" of a cloud is tricky because this word describes the altitude of a cloud's base—the lowest part of a cloud—and not its top. This seemed counterintuitive until I realized that the tops of clouds would be useless for classification purposes. The tops are often obscured by the cloud itself and can change significantly and rapidly as they develop and then dissipate. The base of a cloud, on the other hand, remains relatively more stable during its lifetime. So, if you are trying to determine how high a cloud is, lower your sights and study its base.

This is easier said than done. Depending on your vantage point, your horizon line, and the type of cloud you are looking at, the base of a cloud may not be obvious. I have stood a long while watching distant clouds float toward me and directly overhead and been unable to determine if what I was seeing was a cloud's base, its side, or perhaps its gluteal back end.

The difference between the base and the top of a cloud is most obvious in Cumulonimbus clouds (the "thunderheads") when you can observe them from afar. From a distant vantage point, the bases of these low clouds appear flat and dark gray, their tops bulging and bright white. Do not, as I have done numerous times, point to such a cloud and say, "Look how high that cloud is!" Though its top is, in fact, several miles above the earth, it is still classified as a low cloud. Instead of saying "high," meteorologists would like us to use the word "thick" or "deep" to describe the vertical extent of a cloud—the distance between its base and its top.

"Deep" can be confusing if this word sends your mind downward into a canyon, hole, grave, or the bottom of a lake. I prefer "thick," especially when looking at a towering Cumulonimbus. "Deep" just doesn't sound right.

Now for the numbers.

Low clouds occur between ground level and 6,500 feet, mid-level clouds between 6,500 and 23,000 feet, and high clouds between 16,500 and 45,000 feet.

These numbers are more manageable in kilometers: low clouds occur between ground level and 2 kilometers, mid-level between 2 and 7 kilometers, and high between 5 and 13 kilometers.

These altitudes are even more manageable in words: "low," "mid-level," and "high." There is no shame in avoiding numbers; meteorologists routinely use these terms to describe the level of cloud bases.

Note that both mid-level and high clouds may form between 16,500 feet and 23,000 feet. Though clouds generally stay within their altitude ranges, they seem to scoff at horizontal lines and numbers. Clouds do not know they live in a tripartite sky.

And there is another problem—latitude. The altitude levels I listed above (and use throughout this book) are the ones standardized by the WMO for temperate latitudes, which is where I live. Because the height of the troposphere varies with latitude, the WMO also provides higher altitude ranges for tropical clouds and lower altitude ranges for polar clouds. You may notice that altitude ranges will vary in textbooks, field guides, and websites you consult. These different numbers may reflect different latitudes or be out of compliance with the WMO standard.

Because I am generally more interested in names than in numbers, I focused my study of clouds on their Latin names and not how high they were. I would ask myself if the clouds I was seeing *seemed* low, high, or in between. After several years of cloud watching, I developed a rudimentary sense of low, mid-level, and high, but I rarely apply the numbers. The clouds do not seem bothered by this.

In the Field

At any height, the clouds can be overwhelming, especially if you feel the urgency—as I did—to learn everything about them all at once to make up for lost time. I had to remind myself again and again to simply enjoy watching the clouds and to cut myself some slack on the book learnin' when it felt like a slog. This was not a crash course in meteorology, after all, but the beginning of what I hoped would be an abiding relationship with the clouds.

Surprisingly, the most helpful book I found for helping me identify and name the clouds was Pete Dunne's *The Art of Bird Identification*. In many ways, Dunne's commonsense approach applies as well to clouds as it does to birds. He suggests birders first learn how their field guides are organized, learn the basic family groups of birds, and get a sense of the habitats and seasons in which these birds will appear.

Dunne suggests you start in your backyard. Study the birds you see and note their distinguishing characteristics—color, shape, form, movement. Whatever you do, Dunne exhorts, do not flip through your field guide, match your bird to a photograph, learn its name, check it off your list, then close your book. You will have learned the name of one bird but little about the bird itself.

I use three field guides, each with a slightly different approach and format, that work well in combination: the concise *Peterson First Guides to Clouds and Weather*, by John Day and Vincent Schaefer, *The Met Office Pocket Cloud Book*, by Richard Hamblyn, and my favorite, *The Cloudspotter's Guide: The Science, History, and Culture of Clouds*, by Gavin Pretor-Pinney. This latter book is not formatted like a field guide (as are the other two) but features useful charts, diagrams, and—best of all—full-page, black-and-white woodcuts of the clouds. While woodcutting might strike you as too coarse a medium for rendering the nuances of specific clouds, artist Bill Sanderson has somehow managed to capture the essential qualities of the ten genera in a way the color photographs in the other guides do not.

Like birders learning about the preferred habitats and seasonal movements of their feathered friends, I tried to get a sense of where and when *my* lofty friends would appear—at what height and during which season, time of day, and type of weather.

With my three books and my *Guide to the Sky* poster, I used a kind of triangulation system for identifying clouds. First, I would take a good look at my cloud and notice its most prominent few features. Then I'd consult my poster (I had two copies, one hanging next to my office window and one downstairs on the fridge door) and develop a hunch as to the genus of my cloud. Next, I turned to the woodcuts and charts in *The Cloudspotter's Guide* and then to the photos and text in the other two guides to learn more about the cloud and to turn my hunch into a best guess. Don't expect, as I did, that your clouds will exactly match the ones in your field guides or on your cloud poster. A photograph captures just one of countless iterations of a cloud. A close match is all you can expect. At first I found it frustrating not to have a way to confirm if my best guess was right or wrong and so learn from my mistakes. Eventually, I learned to enjoy guessing, to embrace the uncertainty, and to let go of the need to get the right answer. And I got used to my meteorologist's response—"Poor Maria!"—when I sent him a cloud photo along with my best guess.

Make the same mistakes enough times and you'll stop making them, or you'll do what birdwatchers do when they cannot identify a bird in the field: they call them LBJs—little brown jobs. Typically LBJs are small birds lacking distinctive field marks. They are often well camouflaged, skittish, and hard to track or to get a good, long look at through your binoculars. LBJs vary according to the skill level of the birder but include the many species of sparrows, finches, wrens, warblers, and flycatchers, especially the drabber females. It's okay to call clouds BWJs—big white jobs.

"The problem with clouds," a birder friend told me with a chuckle, "is that their field marks keep changing."

It was true. By the time we pin a name on a cloud, it changes enough to need a new name.

This is part of the clouds' charm and what keeps me coming back for more.

Cloud Survey Question

 How often do you consciously look at or notice the clouds around you?

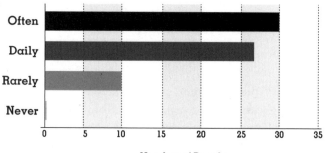

Number of People

Developing the simple habit of looking up takes time. Though I have been watching clouds for several years, I still have to remind myself to look out a window or go outside and look up first thing in the morning. It's all too easy to keep my gaze downward or at eye level, looking just a few feet or yards ahead as I move through the day. I need to look where I was going, but I also need to stop and look up to appreciate the miracles of the sky, to experience the joy of the clouds, and to learn something new about them every day.

The *International Cloud Atlas* notes that a "continuous watch" is necessary for the best observation of clouds, especially those undergoing rapid transition from one form to another.

"A continuous watch" doesn't seem humanly possible. But I wish I could remember to look up more often. It's just not that hard.

VISIBLE

*A cloud is a **visible** mass of water droplets or ice*
crystals suspended in the atmosphere above the earth.

One fair summer afternoon, I set up a lawn chair in my front yard to watch a band of small, tattered white clouds.

That they were visible seemed obvious.

There they were. I saw them.

This was going to be a very short chapter.

But my chair was comfortable and the sun warm. I stayed on, gazing at my clouds, trying to explain to myself why I could see the clouds—or anything—at all. My understanding of light, vision, and the human eye was so rudimentary that I could not create even the simplest of narratives on visibility.

Why Clouds Are Visible

The visibility of clouds is so basic that meteorology books don't even address this topic. They do, however, answer the question of why clouds are white, which is essentially the same as why clouds are visible: because the water molecules in clouds scatter all wavelengths of visible sunlight equally.

This is the standard, reference-book answer.

It is an answer only if you understand it.

I did not.

As soon as my husband (aka Dr. Science) walked in from work, I pounced.

I clenched my fists and positioned them on top of my head like ears on a mouse.

"I am a water molecule," I said. "My head is the oxygen, my fists are hydrogen. Explain to me how water scatters sunlight."

Bless his heart, he put his backpack down and went with it.

He told me that he was the sun. And that sunlight travels through 93 million miles of space—from the sun to Earth—as a stream of invisible oscillating waves of energy. These waves come in different lengths, known as wavelengths, which are measured from the peak of one wave to the peak of the next wave (straight across, not via the trough).

"The wavelengths of light we can see fall in a range known as the visible spectrum and include the colors we know as red, orange, yellow, green, blue, indigo, and violet."

"My fourth-grade pal, Roy G. Biv!" I interjected.

"Isaac Newton, actually. But sure, if that helps. Each color represents a different size wavelength between 0.4 and 0.7 micrometers in diameter. Violet is on the short end, red on the long."

"Wait. Can you refresh me on micrometers?" I asked.

"A micrometer is one millionth of a meter, a thousandth of a centimeter."

I could feel my entire brain squinting as I tried to visualize something this small. Learning later that a micrometer is about one-fiftieth the diameter of a human hair didn't help much. I could only imagine half the diameter of a hair—a split end.

"These colors are visible," my husband continued, "because the cells in the human eye just happened to have evolved to be sensitive to wavelengths in this range. On either side of the visible spectrum is the light we cannot see. Just beyond red you have infrared. Just beyond violet you have ultraviolet. Are you with me?"

"Yes—ish. It all sounds familiar."

"Sunlight enters our atmosphere where it begins encountering various molecules—mostly nitrogen, oxygen, carbon dioxide, and water. Depending on the size of these molecules, the different wavelengths bounce off them differently. When short wavelengths—the blue, indigo, and violet—hit small molecules like nitrogen and oxygen in the upper atmosphere, they scatter away from our eyes. That's our blue sky. When they hit larger molecules like water, they scatter in all directions, including toward our eyes. That's white clouds."

Then my husband told me his left arm represented the long wavelengths (red, orange, and yellow) and the fingers of his right hand were shorter wavelengths (blue, indigo, violet). And then long-wave left arm collided with the hydrogen molecule atop my head and "scattered" off one way; his wiggling "short-wave" fingers bounced off my other hydrogen molecule and went the other way.

It was an absorbing evening, to say the least.

Our molecular pantomime left many questions unanswered, so the next day I tried to work out things on paper. How could sunlight and plain old water make white clouds *and* dark clouds *and* rainbows? Did the sunlight enter the water molecule and then scatter or did it just bounce off the outside of the molecule as my husband suggested? If it just bounces off the outside of it, why did the size of the water molecule matter? What exactly was the water molecule doing to the sunlight when they encountered each other?

With a blue crayon, I outlined a single puffy cloud on a page in my notebook. Using the side of the crayon, I colored the entire sky blue. I left the top right corner (where else?) for the sun. Using a yellow crayon, I drew a solid yellow disc with long pointy rays aiming at the cloud. When I pulled out a few reference books to add more detail, I discovered I had it all wrong.

Pure sunlight is not yellow, and it does not it emanate in lines or triangular rays.

Pure sunlight is white and moves in invisible waves.

This makes the sun difficult to depict accurately with crayons or any medium. Yet from the time we can hold a crayon we draw a yellow sun with distinctly visible rays. There are a few reasons for this. First, yellow is easier to see on white paper. Second, the sun does, in fact, appear yellow when it shines through air molecules, dust, and other particles in the atmosphere (which is most of the time). From high elevations and altitudes, the sun appears less yellow and more white because it is traveling through less of the atmosphere.

Third, we depict a sun with pointy rays because that's how the sun appears in photographs and when we look directly at the sun with our naked eye (which we shouldn't do). These rays do not actually exist. They are optical phenomena caused by the way the iris of our eyes and camera lenses work; both these apertures distort incoming light. The perception of rays may also come from the phenomenon of "crepuscular rays," the light that sometimes shines through the gaps in the clouds, especially when the sun is low in the sky.

Fourth, we use the word "ray" because it sounds like the right word to use. After all, sunlight is a type of energy known as electromagnetic radiation, solar radiation, radiation, or radiant energy. These words are related to the triangular "ray" etymologically and phonetically but not morphologically.

To create a cloud I had to abandon the quaint, culturally accepted, and enduring symbol of the sun, and reimagine sunlight.

I turned the page in my notebook and picked up a yellow crayon. I drew a circle but left its interior white this time. I drew the outline of a cloud in blue. I did not bother with the sky. Between the sun and the cloud I drew seven parallel wavy lines close together. Each line was a different color, from red to violet: Roy G. Biv. Each represented a different wavelength. I labeled the bundle of lines "White Light" even though it was full of color. (That white light was composed of several constituent colors was proven by Isaac Newton in a series of experiments he conducted with glass prisms between 1666 and 1672. Although nearly 350 years have passed since Newton's discovery, I was happy to rediscover this "celebrated phenomenon of color" on this morning.)

I extended each of my colored lines into the cloud and then turned them loose to make left turns, right turns, downturns, upturns, U-turns, slight bends, squiggles, doglegs, and jaunty-angled lines. Each turn represented a deviation in the original trajectory of a wavelength as it entered the cloud and encountered a water molecule. My Crayola-colored cloud was a frenzy of deviations.

In scientific parlance, these deviations are referred to as reflection, diffraction, and refraction. You may not know them by these names, but you have likely witnessed all of them.

When you have looked into a mirror or pool of still water, you have noticed light being reflected: bounced off the mirror or water at the same angle it strikes it.

If you have seen a blurry moon, you have witnessed light being diffracted, or bent slightly, as it passed around the ice crystals or water droplets in a thin layer of cloud between you and the moon.

If you have been amused by the apparently broken drinking straw near the surface of your glass of water, you have observed light being refracted, or bent slightly as it passes from one transparent medium to another (from air to water in this case).

Memorizing these confusingly similar terms isn't important, but knowing that all of these deviations occur simultaneously and constantly in a cloud is. In fact, most meteorologists don't track all the individual deviations of light within a cloud. They refer to what a cloud does to light more generally: scattering.

The sky is blue because air molecules—mostly nitrogen and oxygen—do not scatter sunlight equally. These molecules scatter sunlight *preferentially*. When sunlight strikes nitrogen and oxygen molecules, the shorter blue wavelengths present in the sunlight are scattered and make the sky appear blue to our eyes. (The wavelengths we might see as indigo and violet have been scattered earlier and higher in the atmosphere and are essentially "behind" or "above" a relatively thick band of sky-blue sky.)

What the water droplets in clouds do to visible sunlight is *equal* or *non-preferential* scattering. What this means is that short, medium, and long—all wavelengths—are scattered equally. No particular wavelength dominates. White light goes in, white light comes out—unlike the sky around the clouds.

In order for a cloud to be visible we must be able to see it with our naked eye. In the back of our eyes, our retinas contain light-sensitive cells—rod-shaped cells (known as rods) and cone-shaped cells (known as cones). When the cloud-scattered sunlight reaches these cone cells, they fire off a message via the optic nerve that reaches our brain. The brain produces the sensation of a color we call white.

We see the clouds by day because the cone-shaped cells give us vision in bright light and are sensitive to the specific wavelengths in white light. We also see clouds at night because the rod-shaped cells give us vision in dim light and allow us to see shades of black, white, and gray.

Not all clouds are pure white, of course. They can also hold shades of white, gray, and every color present in sunlight. The presence of these non-white colors is related to the size, shape, and composition of a cloud as well as its position with respect to other clouds and to the sun. The size of the water droplets, the shape of the ice crystals, and their density within a cloud also change the way light behaves in that cloud. Clouds that are thick or are composed of large liquid water droplets, for instance, often appear gray because they are absorbing more sunlight than they are scattering. Clouds also reflect the varying colors around them. Clouds can reflect the pink and orange colors of the sky near sunrise and sunset. The undersides of clouds can reflect the blue of the ocean, the green of a lagoon, the white of coral sand. Only a few species of our Cirrus clouds are pure white. All the rest of the clouds are shaded or tinted.

Ironically, the more I understood about the visibility of clouds, the more difficult they were for me to watch. While gazing at the clouds, I would superimpose onto them as many individual water droplets as my mind's eye could generate. Then I'd travel 93 million miles to the sun and then bring a big beam of light into the clouds and imagine multicolored wavelengths scattering every which way. My clouds flashed in rainbow colors. My clouds flashed bright white and gray. My clouds vibrated and buzzed with energy. My clouds were exhausting. I felt scatterbrained. I gave up drinking coffee for a while, thinking that the buzz from the caffeine might be jamming some electromagnetic channel of understanding between my brain and the clouds. Some days I couldn't bring myself to look at clouds at all. They were just big billowing reminders of how little I knew. Gone were the happy, innocent days when I saw them simply as dragons and elephants—or ice-cream castles in the air.

Cloud Survey Question

 Can you recall your first memory of watching a cloud?

> *I remember a road trip when I was about ten . . . and I was looking out the window with my sister and I was naming everything I saw in the clouds and let me tell you—I see EVERYTHING in clouds. From hippos to ducks, from princesses to sailboats.*
>
> *I have a memory of lying on my back in the grass on a warm day, looking at the clouds with other kids in the neighborhood. We would describe the cloud shapes in terms of animals.*
>
> *As a young adult, I would lie outside and look at clouds and "make them disappear"—something I had read about in a book. Basically, if you look at a cloud for a long time directly, it does indeed disappear!*

I was about four years old on a road trip with my family to Tennessee. My dad put duct tape in the middle of the seat as a demarcation line between my rival sibling and me. I sat there and stared out of the window as we drove down the interstate, watching cloud after cloud.

[I was] four or five years old. My family loved to go out into the yard and watch thunder clouds and lightning (not necessarily a good idea). This was especially true if tornado watches had been issued.

I was with my parents at Lake George in NY State. I was 7 or 8. We were in a restaurant with a view of the lake and watched a storm front moving over the lake towards us. They were trying to show me the areas where rain was already falling. I was unable to see it because I didn't know what I was looking for.

I was a child when my friend's grandmother pointed to the clouds and said a storm is coming so you'd better run home.

When I was about 7 years old I got my first camera—a Kodak Instamatic. I used to lie on the grass in my back yard and take pictures of the trees and clouds. There was something about the contrast in shapes and patterns that fascinated me.

Probably about the time we moved up to Washington, when you look at the clouds and go, "Oh, the rain's a-comin'."

I was very young. I don't remember where I was, but I was lying flat on my back and squinting into a bright sky. I was more or less alone—probably someone was keeping an eye on me, but no one was really with me. I had recently read a book where someone found shapes in the clouds, and I thought I could too. I found dragons and monsters and dogs and cats and fish and trees and umbrellas and people and a lot of cotton candy and feather pillows. How disappointed I was that some clouds didn't really look like anything.

My first memory of watching a cloud dates back to when I was in elementary school and I spotted a cloud that looked like Richard Nixon in profile. It was 1968, the year Nixon ran for president and was elected, and the newspapers and magazines often depicted him as a caricature with a puffy forehead, bulbous jaws, and swooping nose. This first memory is less about the cloud itself than about my parents having a good laugh when I pointed it out to them.

Noticing familiar shapes in clouds is one of life's simple pleasures and a time-honored introduction to them—a gateway to observing and learning something about clouds. What actually makes them look like dragons, hippos, or fish scales? Why are they dark like Darth Vader? How did they morph—and so quickly—from fish scales to angel hair? Why don't they ever stop raining? Why is it so hard to focus on just one cloud?

The Five-Minute Cloud

One early June afternoon in Olympia I challenged myself to watch a single cloud for five minutes. I hoped to develop a daily habit to help my cloud watching develop into a more focused looking. Five minutes doesn't sound like much of a challenge, but if you don't like to sit still or do one thing at a time, it can be agony.

When a band of tattered little tissue-paper clouds appeared in the southeastern sky, I turned my lawn chair to face them and then set my cell-phone alarm. I focused on just one edge of one cloud but within seconds felt my eyes shifting left and right to other clouds and then to other things flitting about in the space between me and clouds. A robin, a crow, a dragonfly, a glint of light from the top of the maple, a bee, a hummingbird.

Resetting my alarm, I began again, focusing on just one of the tattered clouds. It was hurrying across the sky in an aloof but happy kind of way. I squinted a bit to keep my eye muscles tight and my gaze focused.

The cloud changed shape a little, but nothing really happened—at least nothing revelatory or even noteworthy. What was this cloud? Cumulus? Stratus? Stratocumulus? I had no idea. I glanced down at my cell phone. One minute had passed. I looked back up at my cloud. It was still visible, but it seemed different—smaller perhaps, but it was hard to tell. It floated over my neighbor's house and then disappeared behind a stand of trees. I dashed inside to get my sunglasses, my polarized ones that enabled me to see more of a cloud's depth and its subtle details—its thinnest wisps, its smallest bulges, and even entire clouds otherwise too thin or small to be visible. Back outside, I chose another cloud, farther upwind and higher above the trees, and reset my alarm.

Then I heard voices.

They were not from angels in the clouds. They belonged to friends of my then-fifteen-year-old son. Their voices grew louder as they came up the street, skateboards clattering. Though my concentration was broken, I kept watching my cloud. Soon they were at the edge of my front yard. So as not to appear rude or eccentric, I got up, walked over to them, and said, "Hi. Cool boards." My son came out of the house, and I quickly retreated back to my lawn chair.

When my five-minute alarm went off, I was not in my chair. I was on my hands and knees in my garden, ten feet away, looking down at the beautiful brown dirt, weeding. Something must have distracted me. I had completely forgotten about the clouds. When I looked up at the sky, my clouds were gone.

There are plenty of books on the "art of seeing" but none so perfectly—and uncannily—addressed my problems of seeing the clouds as a book of art and literary criticism by British novelist Jeanette Winterson. In *Art Objects: Essays on Ecstasy and Effrontery*, Winterson describes four problems that arise when she challenges herself to look at one painting in an art gallery for one hour and with no distractions.

> *Increasing discomfort. When was the last time you looked at anything, solely, concentratedly, and for its own sake? Ordinary life passes in a near blur. . . . We find we are not very good at looking.*

> *Increasing distraction. Is my mind wandering to the day's work, to the football match, to what's for dinner, to sex, to whatever it is that will give me something to do other than to look at the painting?*

> *Increasing invention. After some time spent daydreaming, the guilty or the dutiful might wrench back their attention to the picture. What is it about? Is it a landscape? Is it figurative? More promisingly, is it a nude? . . . I can make up stories about the characters on the canvas . . .*

> *Increasing irritation. Why doesn't the picture do something? Why is it hanging there staring at me?*

Ultimately, Winterson concludes, a painting objects to the viewer's "lack of concentration" and "failure to meet intensity with intensity." Winterson could have been writing about clouds. Stare at a cloud for even five minutes and you will inevitably experience the progression of problems she describes. You'll feel disappointment in the clouds and in yourself.

The antidote to these problems, Winterson suggests, is simply to "make the experiment again (and again and again)," to work at meeting "intensity with intensity" so the painting (or cloud) doesn't object to your lack of concentration.

It took me several weeks of daily cloud-watching experiments to notice any progress. And then one morning—after a succession of five-minute failures with a fleet of small, flat clouds—a small victory. I settled my gaze on one cloud, small and flat like all the others that morning. But this one had depth. Had my cloud suddenly "puffed out," or was I just now noticing its cotton-ball shape? Why was it suddenly expanding and contracting as if it were breathing? My focus sharpened, and I felt a little boost of adrenaline. Around the edges of my cloud, delicate wisps furled and unfurled like octopus tentacles in a 3-D movie. It roiled and churned. Though it was clearly moving gradually to the east, parts of it appeared to surge westward. The wisps moved in every direction, as if they were being poured out from the center of the cloud. Then the cloud got smaller and thinner and began coming apart. Now it was several clouds, then wispy fragments—smaller and paler—and then nothing.

My cloud was gone. Just like that.

Astonished, I kept my gaze on the empty patch of blue sky. My heart raced. My throat was dry. I had just witnessed—for the first time in my life—a visible cloud becoming invisible. Meeting intensity with intensity had nearly undone me.

When my five-minute alarm sounded, I startled. I had forgotten where I was. I wasn't sure where my body began and ended. My watching had become seeing, and then my seeing had become something else. Something more full-bodied and fluid. Something like breathing.

Stratus

That five-minute cloud, I would later discover, was a Stratus cloud. Stratus clouds are the lowest of the ten cloud types, with their bases occurring from ground level to 6,500 feet above it, though they rarely occur above 3,000 feet. These are common in the Pacific Northwest, both east and west of the Cascade Range. Being the lowest of the low clouds, Stratus are the easiest to see and examine up close. I was thrilled to discover that much of what I could observe in Stratus clouds could be applied to other clouds at higher altitudes where these features are less obvious or impossible to detect. Stratus have much in common with other layered clouds—Nimbostratus, Stratocumulus, Altostratus, and Cirrostratus—and it helped me to imagine these clouds as Luke Howard might have, as higher, thicker, or icier "modifications" of Stratus.

Stratus clouds are gray, water-droplet clouds with uniform bases and may produce a fine misty rain (drizzle) or snow. Stratus clouds can be opaque (Stratus opacus) and block the sun; they can be translucent (Stratus translucidus) and appear like gauze. They can appear as a featureless layer (Stratus nebulosus); they can be separated and appear as small patches (Stratus fractus). This latter was the species of Stratus that had made my heart race—the bright, white cloud that has brought more joy into my cloud-watching life than any other cloud.

Unfortunately, most field guides and cloud-watching books describe Stratus in a pejorative way: "formless," "grayish," "ugly," "undefined," "diffuse and rather dull," "indistinct," "and "profoundly unpoetic." One meteorology textbook offers this: "What distinguishing features enable us to identify Stratus clouds? The answer is—no distinguishing features."

This may be true of some species and varieties of Stratus clouds, especially if you are interested in pointing out familiar shapes in the clouds or intent on being a cloud curmudgeon. I consider a blanket a shape and flying tissue paper completely dazzling. I love Stratus clouds for trying so hard in the face of the billowing Cumulus and ethereal Cirrus clouds that usually steal the show.

Stratus clouds form when a layer of warm, moist air encounters a layer of colder air and is forced to rise over it. As the warmer air rises, it cools, condenses, and forms a cloud. Stratus can also form when a layer of warm, moist air drifts over a cooler surface, such as the ground, an ocean, or a lake.

When the base of a Stratus cloud touches the earth (ground or water), it is known as fog. Fog is the lowliest of Stratus clouds. Fog is not technically a species or variety in the Stratus genera, and it does not have an official Latin name. You could describe fog as Stratus nebulosus or Stratus opacus, but I don't advise it. You will get blank stares, which will require you to say "fog" afterward to make your meaning clear.

Fluent in Fog

"Fog" is a clunky name for a cloud, especially one so delicate and ethereal. Meteorologists have added polysyllabic adjectives to describe the main types of fog—advection, radiation, frontal, mixing, upslope, and valley—but most of us rely on just five words to describe fog: "thick," "dense," "heavy," "patchy," and "light." Can't we do better?

In fact, we have done better. A gleaning by one person (me), in one language (English), from easily accessible resources (my small collection of weather books and chanced-upon websites) yielded dozens of names. Some are official, others vernacular, many nicknames.

Some names are derived from where they occur: London fog, California fog, ground fog, valley fog, upslope fog, hill fog, high fog, marine fog.

Some are named for their attributes: acid fog, black fog, dry fog, flash fog, force 10 fog, frozen fog, freezing fog, killer fog, rime fog, and stink fog.

Other names allude to how the fog forms: advection fog, caribou fog, evaporation fog, frontal fog, ice fog, mixing fog, precipitation fog, radiation fog, steam fog, and supercooled fog.

Others still are named for a shape: fog streamer, fog bank, fog belt, fog bow.

And then there are the nicknames: Antarctic sea smoke, arctic sea smoke, arctic mist, air hoar, frost flakes, frost smoke, pea souper, pogonip, sea mist, sea smoke, smog, steam devil, and water smoke.

One of my favorite names is "pogonip," the word for a dense frozen fog that forms in the deep mountain valleys of many western states. The word is derived from a Shoshone word *payinappih*, which means "cloud." I knew this word was the proverbial tip of the iceberg of words for clouds in Native American languages, but, as tempted as I was to explore, I returned to my native tongue.

"Pea souper" struck me as a quaint and colorful British name for the particularly thick fog common in London and elsewhere in the UK. I imagined a long walk through a foggy moor and a comforting bowl of hot soup until I learned of the fog's darker side. This benign and naturally occurring fog turned toxic during the Industrial Revolution when the water droplets in the fog formed around sulfur dioxide and the soot belched from coal-burning factories and fireplaces. In 1905, the resultant "pea soupers" were dubbed "smog"—a name that combines "smoke" and "fog." By the middle of the twentieth century, automobile exhaust and other airborne pollutants had made London's smog thicker, more persistent, and increasingly dangerous to human health. In December 1952, a layer of smog hung over London for five days, reducing visibility to less than ten feet, bringing traffic to a standstill, and making it difficult for area residents to breathe. The Great Smog of 1952, as it is known in history books, killed an estimated twelve thousand people from respiratory failure and caused widespread coughing, choking, bronchitis, and lung inflammation.

Naturally occurring fogs can also prove menacing when they occur in the "wrong" location. California's broad, 450-mile-long Central Valley is the home of a wintertime fog known as tule fog, named after a type of bulrush plant called tule (pronounced *too*-lee), which grows in the valley's wetlands where these fogs typically form. Tule fog can build to 1,700 feet thick, reduce visibility to nearly zero, and last for weeks. This wouldn't be such a problem unless you built a highway through such a foggy valley, as was done. Tule fog has become the leading cause of weather-related traffic accidents in California. In 2009, the California Department of Transportation completed a $12-million fog-detection and fog-warning system on a thirteen-mile stretch of Highway 99 through the valley south of Fresno. It's too bad we speed through fog in our cars rather than stand in its beauty like the caribou do.

"Caribou fog" forms in places such as Greenland when large herds of caribou exhale warm, moist breath into the cold air. Fog forms and lingers over the herd, perhaps protecting them from detection by predators. Though I have never read of "elk fog," I have seen herds of these caribou-like creatures in the Pacific Northwest grazing in the morning fog. I may have to propose a new cloud species name, Stratus cervus, based on the Latin name for elk.

More common in the Pacific Northwest is advection fog, which forms when warm, moist air is carried, or "advected," over an area of cooler water— such as over coastal waters. Cape Disappointment, in Washington's southwest corner, is ranked as the foggiest place on the Pacific Coast thanks in part to advection fog. More famous is the advection fog in San Francisco Bay, where it develops thickly and so photogenically around the Golden Gate Bridge.

Radiation fog is also common in the Pacific Northwest, especially on fall and winter days when our skies are clear, nights are long, the air is calm, and the Pacific storm season isn't yet in full gear. Radiation fog can also appear after long periods of rain followed by a clearing at night. During such times, the ground radiates its heat into space at night and cools. The air in contact with the cooled ground also cools, and, if that air is sufficiently moist, the water in it condenses and forms droplets of liquid water. On some mornings, we might wake to see dew or frost on the ground. On other mornings, when the layer of moist air is deeper (thicker), we may wake to see fog above the ground.

What is the difference between fog and mist? They both form the same way, but the general rule is that if visibility is reduced to less than 1,000 yards, it's fog. If visibility is greater, you are looking at mist. Mist is easy to confuse with haze, but haze is composed of very small particles of dust, sea salt, or other particles that are suspended in the air. Haze isn't water at all.

In Olympia, fog can appear any time of year, but is most common in late summer and early fall. Thick, dense fog can obscure whole sections of the city, slow traffic on streets, and cause multiple-car accidents on the highways. Thin, patchy fog creates a dreamlike atmosphere in forest and field. It softens hard lines and takes the edge off time with its gentle, nebulous caress. Fog is a cloud, yes, but something else too. Fog is as integral to my local landscape as the water and inlets of Puget Sound, glacial-carved lakes, Douglas firs, great blue herons, bald eagles, Interstate 5, and views of Mount Rainier.

Around the autumn equinox, fog has a special magic. Every morning is noticeably darker, every night a little cooler. There is nothing the earth can do about it. Resigned, it simply lets go and releases its summer into the autumn air. But not all at once, instead slowly, over weeks, in a series of long exhalations. On still, cool nights I sense that our tired, end-of-summer earth is sighing. In the morning there is the beautiful blanket of fog it has exhaled.

A Swim in the Stratus

Fog is the only cloud you can swim in, though no one mentions this fact or recommends this simple, rare pleasure.

One September morning, the fog looked like my sleep felt: dreamy, cozy, and seductive. I could have stayed in bed another hour, but I had been watching the clouds for nearly a year and it was time to experience a cloud up close.

I left my warm bed, dressed, and slipped out the front door just before seven o'clock.

Visibility was poor and perversely exciting. When I looked down, the ground was clear twenty feet from where I stood. When I looked straight out, the house across the street was more apparition than architecture, a house you might see in a movie flashback or dream sequence. The great Douglas firs, redcedars, and hemlocks around the house had been truncated by the fog; the stoutness of their trunks was the only clue to their hundred-foot heights. The fog was even thicker farther down the road. The paved black street was invisible, the houses were mere rooflines. The fog had washed the color out of everything.

I expected to be engulfed by this thicker fog as I walked down my street, but everything came into sharper focus instead. How disappointing. I thought I could somehow escape my twenty-foot circle of visibility. Perhaps if I kept walking, I'd find my way into foggy obscurity.

The nearby middle-school soccer field was reduced to a green patch of grass surrounding the white framework of the goal at one end. A dozen or so crows and white-and-gray gulls gathered in an uneasy flock, apparently stranded by the fog. The only sound accompanying this strange tableau came from the wet street beyond the field—from the cars passing invisibly with an attenuated whoosh.

I could still see my hand in front of my face and, much to my amazement, a swarm of specks—actual visible water droplets—floating between my eyes and my hand. The singular fog became a plurality of visible grayish-white droplets that floated and pulsed in wisps around me. What was causing them to pulse—a slight breeze? My breath? The movement of my body? I held my breath and kept very still. The fog shifted a bit to the left and then the right. I stood for several minutes, looking around and deeper into the fog over the field and above me. The fog seemed to be thinning around me and thickening at the far end of the soccer field. As I walked in that direction, the fog thinned and receded as I approached. This was a playing field; the fog was not only playing tricks on my eyes but also giving me chase.

I was game. I'd outsmart the fog. I ran to the left several yards, then right, then left again but always found myself at the thin edge. Even when I ran greater distances and in different directions, the fog receded at my pace. I couldn't get in the thick of it. I was trapped in visibility.

Suddenly I was not alone.

Headlights appeared in the fog. Cars were pulling into the parking lot adjacent to the field—parents dropping their kids off for school. I slunk away bested—but not defeated—by a cloud. Zero visibility had to be somewhere this morning.

I returned home and then set out by car for a tiny hilltop park with a territorial view that takes in Olympia, Puget Sound, the Olympic Mountains, and Mount Rainier. The morning rush-hour traffic was slow and surreal. Visibility had worsened with added glare from car headlights shining into the fog and tailpipe exhaust.

The fog thickened over the Deschutes River but thinned considerably as I drove up a long, steep hill. Patches of blue sky appeared. The sun sparkled so brightly on the black pavement that I had to squint to see. Suddenly I was driving under a perfectly clear blue sky.

What a rip-off.

An elevation change of just over a hundred feet was enough to ruin my date with the hilltop fog.

Disappointment turned to joy at the park overlook. Below, a thick and rumpled blanket smothered the city and the inlets and islands of lower Puget Sound to the north. There was no state capitol dome, no government buildings, no town whatsoever. The forested hills around the city had vanished too. Not even the tips of hundred-foot Douglas firs poked up through the fog. Olympia was socked in.

I hunkered down at a picnic table to wait for the fog to envelope me as it lifted. I sat there an hour. The fog did not lift. Instead it moved southward as if being sucked inland by a giant vacuum. Then the fog began to thin at its trailing edge. The city began to emerge—the capitol dome, the construction cranes, the tops of trees.

Naturally I panicked.

"No!" I shouted. "This cannot be happening!"

The fog was going to vanish before I had a chance to embrace it. I wanted to be *in* the fog, not above it. I'd have to pursue it inland. But where? A low spot? A river valley? A quarry? A lake?

I lived less than a mile from a nine-acre, 65-foot-deep lake gouged out when the Vashon Glacier retreated fifteen thousand years ago. Our landscape is full of these lakes, known as kettle lakes, glacier lakes, or pothole lakes. The clouds fill them with rainwater from above; natural springs feed them from below. My neighborhood lake is a popular fishing and swimming spot in summer. On this cool September morning, I'd likely have it all to myself.

I drove out of the sunshine, down through the still-thick layer of fog into my neighborhood and back to my house. My husband had left for work and my sons for school. I changed into my bathing suit, terry-cloth robe, and flip-flops. I left a note on the kitchen table: "At the lake—back around 9!" It was a courtesy note of sorts for my family—or the 911 dispatcher, just in case. I was certain I'd return and throw out my note before anyone had a chance or need to read it. I swam in the lake regularly and knew the contours of its shoreline well. Second thoughts seeped in anyway.

Would fishermen be on the lake? Would they run over me in their motorboats or rescue me if I needed it? Or both? What if the fog was so thick that I became disoriented and swam around in circles? What were the warning signs of hypothermia? I could panic, cramp, and drown. My sons wouldn't be home from school until three o'clock and might not see my note. It could be near dark before they came into the kitchen, hungry, and noticed something missing: dinner. Oh, and Mom.

There is a standard list of "ten essentials" to pack when hiking in the wilderness (map, compass, water, extra food, flashlight, etc.), but I knew of no such list for swimming in the fog. As I was thinking about a safety net, the image of a thin, white cotton string—the kind used for tying up brown paper packages or flying a homemade kite—came to mind. I found some in the rusty toolbox in our garage, wound messily around a short cardboard tube. I put the string in one pocket of my robe. I put my driver's license, medical insurance card, car keys, and cell phone in the other. I left a phone message for my husband. I was all set. This was going to be great.

At the crest of the hill leading down to the lake, I felt a smile stretch across my face. There was no lake. There were no docks, no boats, no lakefront houses. It was all fog. All fog except for the wide cement slabs of the public boat ramp. And the brown, wooden fishing regulation sign. And the pickup truck.

The truck was parked at the left edge of the gravel parking lot, facing the lake, its engine running. The man in the front passenger seat was reclining, perhaps sleeping. There was no one in the driver's seat. The driver must be on the lake fishing, I thought. I'd have to keep my head above water and be prepared to shout, wave my arms, or dive if his boat got too close. I parked across the lot from the truck and stepped into the bracing air.

Because a middle-aged woman approaching a fog-covered lake at this (or any) hour might be interpreted by a guy in a truck (or anyone) as a bit weird or possibly suicidal, I decided it would be considerate (to him) and prudent (for me) to explain what I was doing. I started toward the truck but stopped when I noticed that the man's eyes were closed.

From the edge of the lake, I could see about fifteen feet across its surface. I wasn't sure how far the middle of the lake was from the shore, but I knew it took about ten minutes of steady overhand crawl to get there.

I hung my robe over the fence, grabbed my string, and stepped onto the first of the submerged cement slabs of the boat ramp. I was in—ankle-deep, committed, and covered in chill bumps. The water temperature was probably around 65°F.

I listened for the putter of a fishing boat. There was only silence, the fog, and the lake.

My feet now numb, I waded in up to my thighs and over to the post of a chain-link fence jutting partway into the lake, dividing public property from private. I tied the end of my string to the post and waded in to my waist. The worst part was over. I held the cardboard tube of string above my head and leaned all the way back. The water wrapped around my shoulders like a warm blanket. The water was actually warmer than the air.

I kicked away from the shore on my back, releasing my string inch by inch. Soon my white cotton lifeline sagged in an arc between me and the fence post. When the fog obscured the fence post, I began to laugh. There I was, alone on the lake, holding a string now only theoretically tethered to the post. I gave my string a tug. I felt safe and happy and could not imagine feeling otherwise.

I alternated kicking hard to stay warm and treading water to listen for boats. The lake was silent. There were no sounds from Canada geese, mallards, or osprey. None from fishermen or triathlon-bound swimmers in wetsuits. Not a shout, a cough, or a splash. It was just me under a strange celestial dome of fog and surrounded by water moving in concentric rings away from my body. Soon I'd be in the middle of the lake and in the middle of the fog.

Too soon my string ran out.

What now?

I had no choice.

I let go of the string.

It floated away, riding toward the shore on my ripples.

Both hands now free, I backstroked and gazed up into the fog. My wet arms stung as I swept them through the fog. This cloud had fangs. Suddenly it occurred to me that all the clouds must feel this way—cold and stinging and not at all cozy as they appear to be. Even the puffy Cumulus sofas must feel like this stinging fog.

I kept my arms under water and frog-kicked for a while. To stay warm (and to amuse myself), I executed some dramatic, pointy-toed, Esther Williams kicks. Puffs of fog swirled around me as I splashed summer-warmed water into the cool autumn air. What a strange and wonderful little universe. I was in my own cloud, relaxed. Until I remembered the man in the truck.

What *was* he doing there in the parking lot? Where was the driver? And why was the engine running? And then it struck me. Why hadn't I bothered to look to see that the exhaust pipe wasn't sending a cloud of deadly fumes into the truck? What was I doing lolling around in the fog when I could be saving a life? Turning, I swam quickly toward the shore, and then I stopped and treaded water. Was I creating drama where there was none? Guy sleeping, woman swimming. It was that simple. Everything was probably okay. I headed back toward the center of the lake.

Probably okay? Treading in the murky waters of personal responsibility, I could no longer focus on the fog. Once more I turned to the shore.

Just shy of the boat ramp, I could see that the man in the truck was sitting upright and moving. Relieved, I waded toward the fence to retrieve my string—my once-taut lifeline now shortened into a series of lazy meanders and floating among the cattails. I broke the tight wet knot, gathered the string into a sloppy tangle, and walked up the boat ramp out of the lake. Averting my eyes from the truck, I put on my robe and flip-flops and got into my warm, dry car.

I made a U-turn to leave the parking lot—a turn that brought my car right alongside the truck. As I drove slowly past, our side windows were lined up for a few seconds. The man and I glanced at each other.

I gave a little wave.

He gave a little wave back.

We both smiled—alive and awake—no questions asked, no explanations needed.

Fogged In

A few weeks after my swim, I rented a friend's studio apartment on the northern outskirts of Olympia near Woodard Bay. My plan was to write there from Monday to Friday, away from the distractions of home, where I usually work. The studio had French doors that looked onto a farm with a red barn, a few grazing horses, and undulating fields backed by Douglas firs. And above the trees: a generous view of the sky. There was just one problem: clouds.

They were so distracting. Too often I was torn between writing about clouds and watching them. What was more important, I asked myself, a sentence I was crafting or the clouds' glorious phrasing of water and sunlight? Time and again, clouds prevailed. Like today. Now. I looked out through those French doors I should have curtained and into the thick fog that had settled overnight on the fields. It showed no signs of going anywhere, but I kept my eyes on it, knowing it had to "lift" or "burn off" eventually.

Why use quotation marks around "lift" and "burn off"? Because, while those terms are common, fog neither lifts nor burns off, though that is what it appears to be doing. Fog mostly evaporates from beneath. How does this happen when the sun is shining down on the top of the fog? No matter how thick the fog, the heat from the sun can always penetrate it and reach the ground, and as the ground beneath it warms, the air in contact with the ground warms too. That warm air rises below the fog. As the underside of the fog layer warms, the fog droplets evaporate, changing from visible liquid droplets to invisible water vapor. The top of the fog rises too but less noticeably, and it evaporates as it mixes with the warmer air above it.

I had never watched a foggy day turn into a sunny one, and the morning weather report forecast sun by early afternoon. I put on my coat, pulled my chair outside, and settled in to watch the show.

The fog obscured the distant trees, red barn, farm fields, and everything farther than about fifty feet away from me at ground level. Closer in, the fog surged gently over the bent grasses and corn-stalk stubble in the field. A small flock of Canada geese grazed contentedly and then, for no apparent reason, rose in panic and honked their way across the grayness, low to the ground, to settle in a different part of the field.

I wished the fog would do something dramatic, get on with the show. I was getting cold. After another half hour of no drama, I stomped through the field toward the Chehalis Western Trail—an old railroad line turned into a paved recreation path. As I walked southward down the path, the young trees formed a long tunnel. Normally the far end of the tunnel was visible. Today the tunnel just led deep into the fog.

A man emerged from the tunnel and was walking toward me. He was dressed head-to-toe in camouflage, but I saw him anyway. He was very tall, and he was walking a small dog. As we approached each other, I gave a little wave hello.

The man stopped, swept his arm around gesturing at nothing in particular, and asked me how I liked the fog.

I said I loved it.

"You know," he said, "you could tell people you were out walking in a cloud today."

I said I would.

I walked a while longer, then turned back and returned to my chair. Now I could see farther across the field and higher up the trunks of the trees. Looking up, I expected to see a ceiling of fog. Instead the fog was curdled and clumped into cloud-like white and dark gray masses. Between the masses: blue sky.

No longer surging languidly, the clouds above flew past, spiraling out-ward and curling in on themselves at the same time. The patches shrank and thinned as they hurried past, one after the next. They were both exploding and imploding. I half-expected to hear the clouds hissing, screeching, roaring, or thundering with all this commotion. There was only silence.

I stood up out of my chair. Sitting seemed wrong and somehow disre-spectful. These clouds deserved full attention and a standing ovation.

The sun shone more brightly, the fields deepened, the evergreens soared again to their full height. I stared at the still trees and pushed the clouds to the periphery of my vision. After a few minutes, I focused on the clouds again. The trees seemed to sway and the ground to fall away in a dizzying swirl. I had to shut my eyes and to reach for my chair to keep from losing my balance.

Sitting back down, I saw the fog with new eyes. The base had evaporated from beneath, and what was left was the top of the fog layer—the part you would look down on from above. With its base clearly out of touch with the ground and visibility almost normal, my fog was no longer fog. On this day and in this place, it had risen to become a low Stratus, a glorious iteration of fog, a beautiful and—no matter what the critics say—a profoundly poetic cloud.

What I saw and felt of Stratus clouds at ground level helped me understand what was happening with other clouds. In many ways, the other clouds were "Variations on a Theme of Stratus." I could take a field of thick, gray fog and raise it up several thousand feet into the sunlight and make it whiter. I could thicken it and make rain like Nimbostratus. Or I could lift the Stratus clouds and curdle them into Stratocumulus and then lift these even higher to become Altocumulus.

Now that I had seen the cloud droplets in the fog, it was easier to imagine similar droplets inside every cloud. It was just a matter of adjusting their size or density or freezing them into ice crystals to create other clouds. I knew the real processes of cloud formation were infinitely more complicated than this, but for the first time in my life I felt the clouds were letting me in on some of their secrets.

MASS

*A cloud is a visible **mass** of water droplets or ice crystals suspended in the atmosphere above the earth.*

Though "mass" has many meanings, the best fit for a cloud comes from the *Oxford English Dictionary*: "a dense aggregation of objects having the appearance of a single, continuous body."

The "objects" in a cloud are primarily water molecules, billions of them, aggregated into liquid droplets and ice crystals, billions upon billions of them, further aggregated into a single cloud or cloud formation.

The density of this aggregation varies with the type of cloud and atmospheric conditions in which they form. According to one estimate, a typical Cumulus cloud contains about four-thousandths of an ounce of water per cubic yard. This is about a marble's worth of water in a space the size of a loveseat. A typical small Cumulus cloud contains over a million pounds of water—a weight equivalent to roughly one hundred elephants.

The "continuous body" that is the mass of a cloud ranges from massive to miniscule, but a cloud's size is deceptive. Cumulonimbus clouds, for instance, can be nearly 8 miles thick. These clouds are massive, and, because they often dwarf other features in the landscape, they appear to be so. The mid-level Altostratus clouds can also be very large, though you wouldn't necessarily know it from standing underneath one. This gray-white layered cloud can be several miles thick and spread out over several hundreds of miles.

Certain types of Cirrus (the familiar mare's tails) can stretch across the sky for hundreds of miles. Scientists may be able to estimate the weight of such thin, ice-crystal clouds, but that number—whatever it might be—would be difficult to comprehend intuitively.

Clouds can appear miniscule too. I have seen distant white clouds so tiny in the blue daytime sky that they look like stars in the night sky. I have seen clouds up close that appeared to be the size of a bandana. Whether by weight or volume, vertical extent or horizontal spread, or density of droplets, the numbers that quantify the clouds are too large or too small to truly imagine. Our perspective warps these numbers further. The distance between cloud and horizon, and between cloud and cloud watcher, makes the mass that is a cloud abstract and practically unknowable.

Cloud Survey Question

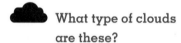 What type of clouds are these?

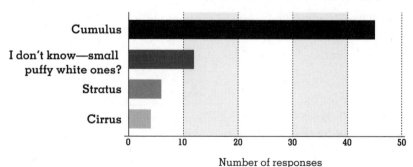

Number of responses

Cumulus

If clouds look like cotton balls, cotton candy, mashed potatoes, cauliflower, hippos, scrunched-up paper towels, or ice-cream castles in the air, they are

Cumulus—"heaped" clouds. They are generally composed of water droplets and are dense with sharp outlines. Cumulus can be bright white and can also be shaded in a rich array of grays, which produce their soft, comfortable-looking shapes. Cumulus clouds are the clouds you've probably imagined yourself napping in or languidly floating in during your eternal rest.

Cumulus are classified as low clouds, with their bases typically at altitudes no higher than 6,500 feet above the earth. When their bases are especially low, I've felt certain I could reach my arm out to touch a Cumulus cloud the way I have heard some very young babies reach out for the moon.

Cumulus are perfect for cloud watchers. They tend to appear during fair weather, which makes for pleasant outdoor cloud-watching conditions, but beware: they can be the small starter clouds for later showers or thunderstorms. Cumulus are isolated or detached clouds separated by blue sky, which makes it easier for you to focus your attention on a single one and not get lost in a horizon-to-horizon mess of layered clouds or a herd of fleecy cloudlets. Cumulus clouds are dynamic and, under certain atmospheric conditions, progress quickly through four distinct and predictable stages, each with a separate species name: fractus, humilis, mediocris, and congestus. From the right vantage point and under certain atmospheric conditions, a cloud watcher can witness a wisp of Cumulus fractus grow into a horizon-eating Cumulus congestus monster in less than an hour.

Watching this Cumulus progression makes for such a soul-satisfying spectacle that it is easy to wonder what could possibly enhance your enjoyment of nature's drama. A little science is what—not enough to spoil the romance but enough to inspire more awe. These Cumulus clouds work hard to look fabulous. It won't kill you to learn a thing or two about their efforts—starting with convection.

Convection

If "convection" is a term you recognize, could define once upon a time, think might be a feature of your new oven, or gives you a strange, sinking feeling—read on.

Convection is a dull name for a fascinating process by which warm air rises, cools, and sinks. This is one process by which clouds—specifically Cumulus and Cumulonimbus clouds (the "convective clouds")—form into visible masses. To fully understand the first part of the convection cycle, the warm air rising part, I set aside my science books and went outside on a cloudless summer morning.

I picked up the morning paper from my driveway and lingered there as the sun was just clearing the tops of the trees. The air was still cool, and long shadows fell across my quiet street, houses, rooftops, green lawns, spiky evergreens, broad-leafed shrubs, and driveways. Most everything in sight was Pacific Northwest green, brown, and gray.

I moved to a spot where my street, driveway, and garden intersected. I slipped off one of my sandals and set my bare foot in a sunny patch on the street. The gray-black pavement was not hot as I expected. It felt close to the temperature of the air. I pivoted around and set the same foot in my tan pebble-and-concrete driveway. It was considerably cooler than the street. The dirt in my garden was much warmer than either the driveway or street. I shifted my weight so the warm earth pressed into my entire sole. It felt really, really good. I shook off my other sandal and stood there in the dirt, thigh deep in yarrow and coneflowers, looking around. Where I had just seen a patchwork of different textures and colors, I now imagined a patchwork of different temperatures—cool, cooler, warm, warmer.

Such patchy, uneven heating happens in every neighborhood, across the landscape, the country, the globe. Every surface the sunlight touches responds to sunlight differently—some surfaces absorb more solar energy than others, some reflect or emit more than others. Because Earth's surface warms unevenly, the air above it warms unevenly too. Why is this so, if the sun shines evenly through the atmosphere before it reaches the earth? The atmosphere, as it turns out, is not very efficient at absorbing heat directly from the sun. Our atmosphere is warmed indirectly by the earth, which absorbs the sun's energy and then radiates it back into the atmosphere. The air near the earth stays cool until the sun-warmed earth warms it. And when that air heats up, it rises.

I have heard all my life that "warm air rises." I know from personal experience that attics are generally hotter than basements, that heat rises out of a chimney, and that hot-air balloons can lift a gondola. But why does warm air rise? In fact, it does not. *Warmer* air rises. A parcel of air that I would consider warm—80°F—will not rise if the air surrounding it is 90°F. The warmer air—the 90°F air—will rise instead. The air that will become a cloud through convection must be warmer than the surrounding air. I'm explaining this distinction not because I am a nitpicker (though I am) but because science textbooks do not explain to literal-minded people like me that "warm" is a relative term and that "warm" really means "warmer."

Warmer air rises because it is lighter than the surrounding air. And why is it lighter? Because, as these same textbooks "explain," lighter air is warmer.

To find my way out of this circular logic, I had to face the fact that I didn't really understand air very well. Though I have been inhaling oxygen and exhaling carbon dioxide all my life, I knew little about this substance that clouds float in. At my age, studying air felt like a demotion, a derailment, another untimely return to yet another square one. But clearly square one was where I needed to go to grasp the meaning of "mass" that is the single, continuous body of a cloud.

Air

"Air" is a simple little word—easy to spell, easy to pronounce—but air is not simple. It is a dynamic and complex mixture of invisible, odorless, tasteless gasses—mostly nitrogen (78 percent), oxygen (21 percent), argon (0.9 percent), and water vapor (between 0 and 4 percent). Second only to water vapor as a variable gas is carbon dioxide (CO_2), at just 0.04 percent.

Air also includes miniscule percentages of naturally occurring gasses I have heard of (neon, helium, ozone, hydrogen, methane) and something I thought was a comic book superhero (xenon). Ubiquitous microscopic particles and pollutants (organic and inorganic, too many to name) increase air's complexity. Air is invisible and remains so unless the density of these particles and pollutants is especially high, and then air appears smoggy, smoky, hazy, or misty.

When sun warms the earth, the air in contact with the earth's surface absorbs some of the earth's heat, and the molecules (of nitrogen, oxygen, water vapor, and others) in that air become excited. Molecules that are "excited" (the actual scientific term) vibrate more rapidly, and, as they do, they move farther apart from the molecules around them, and the air expands.

Imagining all this is easier for me with a metaphor. Science books like to use a balloon, which represents a parcel of air (an imaginary body of air considered separately from the air around it). Imagine a mostly inflated balloon sitting in the sun. As the air inside the balloon warms, the molecules in that air get excited and move apart. This causes the balloon to expand. Now imagine the same scenario without the balloon.

I love to dance (kitchen, husband, wine, R&B), so another metaphor works better for me. Imagine you are hosting a dance party in your home. Your friends are all standing around the kitchen in small groups chatting in a relaxed way. You turn on your favorite high-energy dance music, and your friends suddenly get excited. Feet start tapping, shoulders start shaking, and hips start wiggling. Everyone is soon jiving, bouncing, and dancing around your kitchen, tossing their fleece sweaters and scarves aside as they warm up. Furniture gets pushed aside to make more room. The dancing is contagious, and all your excited friends need more space for their wild dance moves, so they spread out into your hallway and living room. The density of dancers (number of dancers in each room) has been reduced. Because there are fewer dancers in each room, there is less body weight in each room, but the dance party is bigger—it has expanded from a kitchen-sized party to a rockin' house party.

Though molecules also wiggle, shake, jive, and expand, the dance-party metaphor only goes so far. Warmed-up dancers do not float off the ground when they expand, but warmed air molecules do. This lighter (less dense), warmer air rises up over the cooler, denser air around it. The warmer air moves in small wisps and eddies at first. As the sun continues to warm the ground throughout the day, the wisps and eddies will rise several hundred feet above the ground to join other wisps and eddies. As they do so, they converge to form thermals.

Scientists describe a thermal as a "blob," "parcel," "pocket," "bubble," or "column" of rising warm air. You have likely experienced thermals on a bouncy airplane ride when the plane is flying relatively low and slow on takeoff or landing, when the plane is flying over different surfaces. A plane will bounce up over pavement, plowed fields, and homes where thermals are stronger. It will bounce down over the cooler woods, planted fields, and lakes in between them where thermals are weaker.

The shape and size of thermals are somewhat amorphous during their development, though the illustrations in my meteorology textbooks tend to depict them as smooth-sided bubbles or straight-sided columns evenly spaced out across a landscape—too smooth, too straight, and too even-looking based on what I had been reading about the atmosphere. For some clarity, I photographed one illustration of a thermal and emailed it to my meteorologist for his thoughts. He forwarded my email to another meteorologist, a specialist in cloud dynamics, who responded within an hour.

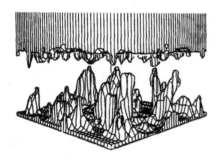

Thermals that form clouds are invisible; while they can be modeled by computer and illustrated as above, I find myself imagining them as the lofty mountains in a classical Chinese landscape painting.

"Those are awful pictures of thermals," he wrote.

He included a diagram of thermals with his email, a diagram based on his numerical modeling studies and sailplane flights through actual thermals. The thermals appeared as very steep and irregularly shaped hills and mountains rising from a flat base. Though the diagram was small and in black-and-white, the contours closely resembled the steep mountains crowded into Chinese landscape paintings.

"Some thermals," the specialist wrote, "are more or less bubbles of buoyant air that rise and expand. Some thermals have long tails and resemble more a jet of buoyant fluid. Sometimes thermals become rotating columns of air which we can see as dust devils or little cyclones of leaves."

With these images in mind, I could—as I stood barefoot in my front yard that morning—see the shape of the air for the first time. My neighborhood was not only houses, lawns, and driveways but also invisible hills, peaks, bubbles, and columns of air expanding, rising, rotating, and jetting their way up into the clear sky. And this was just the first part of the convection cycle, the warmer air rising. The second part—the cooling—made me appreciate water even more.

From the earth's surface up to a little under 7 miles, the temperature of the air in our atmosphere cools with increased altitude. This cooling happens at a surprisingly consistent rate, known as the lapse rate. The standard lapse rate is –3.6°F per 1,000 feet. The air in a rising thermal cools at a different rate—at –5.5°F for every 1,000 feet of altitude. My math (5.5 – 3.6 = 1.9) told me that thermals were doomed to fail unless they got a 2-degree boost. And my meteorology books told me that thermals had a special booster: water.

As the molecules of water vapor in a parcel of rising air cool, they condense. This means they change from vapor to a liquid phase. As each water molecule changes phases, it releases a tiny bit of heat known as latent, or "hidden," heat. This heat is released into the rising air parcel and gives the water molecules a little lift—the boost needed to keep the thermal rising up through the increasingly cooler air.

As the water molecules are condensing, they are also evaporating, changing from liquid to vapor. At a certain temperature, the rate of condensation and the rate of evaporation are in a state of equilibrium. This temperature is known as the dew point. Are clouds dew? Yes, but "dew" is a term reserved for water molecules that condense near ground level and form tiny droplets on blades of grass, leaves, flowers, the hood of your car, and other objects.

Perhaps you have read that "clouds form at dew point," or "when water condenses, it becomes a cloud." Such statements are common but simplify a more dynamic reality. Water molecules are always condensing and always evaporating. Water vapor can become liquid water droplets—cloud droplets—only when the air temperature falls *below* the dew point temperature. At that temperature the rate of condensation exceeds the rate of evaporation, and cloud droplets will form. At this point we may see wisps of whiteness—our Cumulus cloud.

These young wispy clouds are a species of Cumulus known as Cumulus fractus, so named because they appear to be broken off from a larger cloud. In fact, this species appears both in the beginning of Cumulus cloud formation and at the end when larger Cumulus clouds are deteriorating. Cumulus fractus clouds have ragged bases and are often described as looking like wet tissue paper in the sky. They do not sound lovely, but they are, especially when they first form in the clear air. Lovely and also exuberant.

Look: air—warmed and cooled.

Look: invisible water vapor—condensed into visible liquid.

Look: Cumulus—the bright white top of a successful thermal.

Skyline

Witnessing the tiniest visible mass of a Cumulus cloud isn't a matter of checking the sky now and again for some whitish opacity. It helps to be methodical in your study of your local weather conditions (wind direction, dew point, relative humidity, and air temperature) and to check the latest satellite and radar maps. You will need to narrow down your search to a certain quadrant of the sky and window of time when all the conditions are right. Then you can stand in your front yard, scanning the sky, eyes wide open and fingers crossed.

If "methodical" is not the way you do anything, try to accidentally be in the right place at the right time. My happy accident occurred on the Skyline Trail in Mount Rainier National Park one cloudless summer afternoon. My husband and I had stopped to catch our breath after the initial steep ascent from the trailhead. We stood at the edge of the narrow trail above a precipitous drop, careful of our footing as we looked south over a broad and undulating subalpine meadow in bloom, with the serrated Tatoosh Range and the snowcapped peaks of Mount Adams and Mount St. Helens in the far distance. We were breathing in this spectacular vista—not thinking of clouds at all—when a wisp of cloud appeared in front of us, at eye level, and almost within reach. Then it disappeared. My husband and I looked at each other wide-eyed and then turned immediately back to the place where the cloud had been.

"What was that?" I asked.

At first I thought it might have been a puff of smoke or a mirage of some kind. But then it happened again in the very same place. The misty whiteness appeared, quickly spread to the size of a bandana, and then vanished—the leading edge first, followed by the rest. The entire appearance and disappearance took less than five seconds.

We stood there for a few minutes, staring unblinkingly into the clear air, expecting a third wisp—a bigger wisp, a Cumulus fractus that we would watch develop right before our eyes. It never appeared. Perhaps the thermal was too weak, the breeze too strong, or the air temperature off the mark. I felt a twinge of disappointment. "Only two clouds? Where's the third?" Hearing myself say this made me feel greedy and ungrateful. This was the time and place for gratitude, not greed. There I was with my partner in awe—standing on a mountainside and at condensation level no less!—witnessing the entire lives of two clouds.

Development

When the thermals are stronger, Cumulus fractus do persist, develop flat bases at the condensation level, and grow into a larger, more rounded masses known as Cumulus humilis—the "humble" Cumulus, the cloud that is wider than it is tall. Its humility, aesthetically pleasing shape, and association with fair weather has made Cumulus humilis the "classic" cloud, the universal cloud icon, and the cloud kingdom's happy ambassador.

The rounded shape of this stage and later stages of Cumulus is the result of the third part of the convection cycle, the part that cloud lovers often overlook: the sinking air. As a thermal rises, it displaces the colder air above it—the air into which it is rising. The colder, heavier, displaced air sinks around the *outside* of the thermal, where there is little resistance from the rising air. As that colder air sinks and mixes with drier air around it, the liquid cloud droplets in that air warm and evaporate (return to vapor) and leave blue sky around the edges of the thermal.

As a Cumulus cloud develops, the "central" thermal spawns smaller thermals, called convection cells, within the cloud. These cells appear as bulges. With a little patience and polarizing sunglasses (or binoculars), you can easily see these bulges forming, growing, and changing the size and shape of a cloud. Watch a Cumulus cloud closely and you may notice that while the whole cloud moves in the direction of the prevailing wind, parts of it (the bulging convective cells) move in many directions at once. The internet features many excellent time-lapse videos of this. Be forewarned: they are mesmerizing, dizzying, and capable of entertaining you for hours.

My husband and I were canoeing on Ross Lake in the North Cascades one July—my husband in the stern and me paddling steadily, blithely, and watching the Cumulus clouds overhead. It was the perfect time to test part of my explanation of convection.

"You know that Cumulus clouds are isolated clouds, right?" I said.

"If you say so, Boss."

"They are isolated because, as the cold air sinks around the outside of each cloud, the sinking air inhibits the growth of other thermals rising up between the clouds from the ground."

I waited for a reaction. The wait time was longer than usual. I figured my explanation was wrong and that my husband was trying to figure out how to set me straight. I wondered if I should have said "suppresses" instead of "inhibits" or "surface" instead of "ground."

"So basically the sinking air craps on the thermals," he said.

I could not believe my ears.

"What did you say?"

Before he could repeat himself, I began laughing so hard that I could not breathe.

"What's so funny?" he asked.

"Please tell me that Dr. Science did not say that the sinking air craps on the thermals."

My voice came out about two octaves higher than normal, which made me laugh even harder, which made me double over in the canoe, which was not going straight despite my husband's valiant J-stroking.

"That's basically what happens, though, right?" he asked.

"Sure, if that helps, 'Dr. Science,'" I said, using air quotes.

Every time I looked up at the clouds and the blue sky in between them, I'd start laughing again. I pulled the brim of my hat down, eventually regained my composure, and resumed paddling.

If the beleaguered thermals are strong enough, a Cumulus humilis cloud will lose its humble aspect and grow into a Cumulus mediocris—mediocre not because it is ordinary but because it is as wide as it is tall.

The next stage of development, Cumulus congestus, is the largest species of Cumulus, a cloud that might appear singly or as a merged line of several clouds.

A Cumulus congestus is a complex cloud that billows up at different rates from all parts of its spreading base. Cumulus congestus clouds are voluptuous, lusciously lobed clouds whose finely scalloped upper parts are often compared to a cauliflower.

When the top of a Cumulus congestus reaches a certain altitude, the ice crystals, which have been forming in the cloud as it rises through increasingly colder air, begin to give our otherwise rounded cloud a wispy top, one that indicates it has developed into a Cumulonimbus cloud, a convective cloud whose extraordinary features and behaviors earn it a separate genus in cloud taxonomy and a separate section in this book.

However mighty, mediocre, or humble, no individual Cumulus cloud lasts very long. The humilis and mediocris species have a lifetime of ten to thirty minutes. Larger congestus clouds last twenty to forty-five minutes. Why so brief? Atmospheric conditions change, the earth cools, thermals lose their oomph, and strong winds break the convection cycle. In some cases, the shadows cast on the ground by Cumulus and other clouds can cool the earth and sever the connection of the thermals to the clouds. Under such conditions, the clouds' success then brings their downfall.

When Cumulus clouds at any stage dissipate, they thin into wisps and fragments—Cumulus fractus again and briefly—just before evaporating entirely.

If you've been watching Cumulus clouds form and dissipate, you'll experience the Cumulus fractus clouds that mark the beginning and the end of a cloud's life. And you'll know that both stages are equally subtle, spectacular, and poignant.

Look! Clouds!

The more I watched clouds, the more clouds I saw—everywhere. If they were not amassing in the sky, these visible masses were showing up in advertising, in literature, art galleries, stores, and movies where they appeared in a new light—less as meteorological phenomena and more as cultural artifacts.

I noticed that little white clouds floated in blue skies in magazine and newspaper ads for allergy medicines, sleeping aids, eco-friendly homes, and perfect vacation spots. How had these clouds come to symbolize health, happiness, and pollen-free air?

And how had clouds been pressed into service to sell homes? Real-estate ads featured more homes against a backdrop of blue sky and puffy white clouds than against gray skies or even solid blue skies. Somehow these clouds made the houses look happier, cleaner, and more certain to guarantee domestic bliss.

At home-furnishing stores, those same white clouds adorned the sky-blue packaging around most of the bedding, mattress covers, and pillows. Female models in slinky white nightgowns rested their heads on these clouds or dozed comfortably in them. This made no sense. I knew that real clouds were wet, cold, often icy, and unsupportive. The idea of curling up on a cloud for a nap in a white nightie was completely absurd, yet the cloud-covered packaging gave me a cozy and peaceful feeling. Was it because the clouds looked like soft, dry cotton balls or because of a well-forged but twisted link between clouds, heaven, and eternal rest? Whatever the reasons—blatant or subliminal—clouds must boost sales given their ubiquity in the bedding department.

It's not just the ad agencies on Madison Avenue that have co-opted the clouds. Writers in all genres have used the clouds for centuries to mean something other than a mass of suspended water droplets. Bartlett's *Familiar Quotations* contains more than a hundred references to "cloud," "clouds," or "cloudy." Beginning with the Book of Genesis and extending to the poetry of Dylan Thomas, writers quoted in Bartlett's have invoked the clouds to symbolize mystery, inscrutability, unrest, unknowing, confusion, heaven, doom, change, anger, bliss, imagination, vagueness, fertility, peace, freedom, dreams, comfort, and the passage of time.

An online searchable King James Bible reveals clouds employed metaphorically ("whoso boasteth himself of a false gift is like clouds and wind without rain"); meteorologically ("the heaven was black with clouds and wind, and there was a great rain"); and dramatically ("and the Lord came down in a cloud" and "the Lord appeared in the tabernacle in a pillar of cloud"). While Genesis does not mention clouds specifically, some biblical scholars suggest that clouds came into being on the second day of creation. This is when God is said to have created a vault (the sky) to "divide the waters from the waters"—meaning the waters on the earth (ocean, rivers, and lakes) from the waters above it (the rain and therefore, presumably, clouds).

In works of contemporary fiction such as *The History of Clouds*, *The Theory of Clouds*, and *In the Service of Clouds*, clouds are mood setters, plot drivers, meteorological curiosities, and hobbies for sexy protagonists. After several weeks of deciphering David Mitchell's epic novel *Cloud Atlas*, I discovered that it wasn't about clouds at all. Its title refers to a piece of music (composed by a minor player in the book) and is simply evocative, as are the clouds depicted on the book's cover.

Masterminds of information technology use the cloud as the symbol and blueprint for an electronic data storage system. "The cloud" is simply a metaphor—an effective one—for selling a paper-free, CD-free, thumb-drive-free lifestyle. I initially thought that the documents and photographs I stored "in the cloud" went into the atmosphere or ether and had no physical presence whatsoever. In fact, "the cloud" describes an aggregation of enormous computers housed in air-conditioned warehouses, known as server farms, which occupy acres of land on the physical earth. Yet we buy in somehow, accepting the metaphorical power of clouds, believing nothing associated with a happy little cloud could be harmful.

More ominous clouds convey subliminal messages of terror and doom. In newspapers, magazines, and television, images of dark storm clouds appear frequently as the backdrop for advertisements for retirement plans, financial-planning services, and life-insurance policies. Why, I wondered, are nice-looking retired couples in the ads about to be swept up into hurricanes while they are paying their bills? By linking natural disasters (storms, hurricanes, floods) with *personal* disasters (poverty, financial ruin, bankruptcy), advertisers are banking on our innate fear of dark clouds to sell services completely unrelated to the weather.

While visiting art museums in Seattle, Tacoma, San Francisco, and Washington DC, I discovered galleries full of clouds. It delighted me to find clouds in the backgrounds of so many portraits, landscapes, and still-life paintings. Across the centuries, painters have used clouds to suggest a mood, indicate the weather, locate heaven, give cherubs a soft place to cavort, bring drama to a seascape, or add depth to a landscape. Clouds so dominated some landscape paintings I saw—often taking up three-quarters of the canvas— that I wondered why they weren't called "cloudscapes."

My leisurely museum strolls turned into frantic cloud hunts. I'd move from room to room, stopping at a painting only if it had clouds in it. While touring a museum with a friend one day, I stopped in front of the first painting we saw.

"Look! Clouds!" I whispered loudly.

She seemed interested—or at least amused—but by the time we reached the second room, it was clear she was not.

She turned to me and hissed, "Stop it. You are ruining the paintings for me."

I tried to stop, but I just couldn't contain my enthusiasm. We agreed to meet an hour later in the gift shop. When she found me there, I was standing in front of the postcard rack, scanning for clouds to take home as souvenirs.

Increasingly, as I plunged deeper and deeper into the science of clouds, I found myself making regular trips to art museums to look for clouds. In between these trips, I'd head to the public library to stare at the clouds in coffee-table art books. I needed these painted, two-dimensional clouds—clouds that would never rain, snow, develop, dissipate, or do anything at all. These were relaxing clouds unlike the clouds in my textbooks that were used to illustrate meteorological processes I did not yet understand. These were static clouds unlike those outside my window that moved too quickly and behaved in ways I could not yet fathom.

What, I wondered, might a painter teach me about clouds that I could not learn from a textbook, an advertisement, a poem, or from my lawn chair?

Lifting the Clouds

I began looking around for a group of local plein air painters who wouldn't mind my looking over their shoulders while they painted the passing clouds from a meadow, beach, or other picturesque setting around Olympia. I called a talented local artist who taught watercolor painting classes at our local community center. She knew of some groups, but she wasn't in one herself.

"Watercolor paint dries out too quickly outside. Even if you're painting in oil or acrylic, real clouds move too quickly for plein air painting," she explained. "They are too ephemeral."

Of course. I should have known this.

"Why don't you come to one of my Monday morning watercolor classes?" she asked. "I'll do a demonstration of a cloud-painting technique for the whole class. You are welcome to come and watch."

One fine May morning a few weeks later, I packed a notebook, pen, and camera and joined a congenial group of nine students in a sunny second-floor classroom at the downtown Olympia Center. The instructor took a seat at a large table, and we gathered around her—positioning ourselves to get a clear view of the supplies she had carefully laid out: an 11" x 17" piece of thick watercolor paper, several small tubes of paint, four paintbrushes, two jars of clean water, a roll of paper towels, and two 4" x 6" photographs of clouds. One photo featured a band of silvery shaded Cumulus mediocris over low hills dotted with shrubs and clumps of evergreen trees; the other featured a close-up of darker, well-developed Cumulus congestus.

She planned to paint these clouds, from her recent vacation in Yellowstone National Park, and not the clouds I could see out the large classroom window— the young Cumulus humilis floating over the green hills, whose shape contrasted so nicely with the sailboat masts in the marina in the foreground and, I felt, begged to be painted. She saw me looking.

"With reference photos, you paint the clouds you want in the landscape you want. Within reason, of course. You wouldn't paint a low cloud like these low puffy ones on the summit of Mount Rainier, for instance."

She picked up a soft-bristled, wide brush and dipped it into a jar of water. With loose strokes back and forth, she washed her entire paper with the clean water. Next she squeezed out a dab of brownish-yellow paint onto her palette.

"Raw sienna," she announced. "For warmth."

She diluted the paint and then brushed it over the entire paper the way she had done with the water. It was true: paper-white sky took on the warm glow of golden sunlight.

With a mix of diluted raw sienna and burnt sienna, she painted a soft, undulating earth—"something for the sky to rest on," she said.

Raw sienna mixed with cerulean blue gave the hills color—"the green of life," she said.

She brushed the sienna-tinted sky above the hills with a very watery mix of cerulean blue, cobalt blue, and alizarin crimson. At the very top of this wan blue sky she added a band of darker blue—French ultramarine—and then diluted it with a big wet brush as she stroked her way back and forth down the paper. The sky was darker blue at the top, paler blue toward the horizon—"as in nature," she said.

This was true too. The sky does really lighten toward the horizon.

"Now for the clouds," she said. "Remember you have to work quickly while your paint is still very wet."

I leaned in closer to the table.

She did not reach for a tube of white paint but for the roll of paper towels. She tore off a single sheet, scrunched it into a little ball, then pressed it right into the middle of her cerulean sky as if she were blotting up red wine from a white carpet—carefully and with just the right amount of pressure. With a graceful roll of her wrist, she lifted the paper-towel wad to reveal a perfect white puff of cloud. I hadn't seen this coming. She must have somehow hidden a rubber cloud stamp inside the paper towel.

"This technique is called lifting the clouds," she said. "Lifting is a subtractive technique. You lift wet paint off wet paper to expose the white paper beneath. It is one way to paint clouds. You can use white paint—that's an additive technique—but you have to wait until your paper is completely dry or you'll get muddy clouds."

She pressed and lifted her scrunched-up paper towel across her paper to create what appeared to be a living, breathing cloud. It was a Cumulus congestus, one that bulged naturally above the landscape of green hills and invisible thermals.

Suddenly I saw the water in these clouds in a new way. I had always thought of water simply as something artists used to dilute their paints or clean their brushes, but now it was an essential ingredient, perhaps the only ingredient, that could mimic on paper its cloud-forming role in the atmosphere. In art, water could be lifted by absorption to create Cumulus clouds. In nature, water could be lifted by convection to create them. Both processes—marvelous and strange—yield similarly pleasing results.

As I looked at the watercolor clouds in front of me, applause seemed in order, but the demo wasn't over.

"Painting a cloud," she said, "makes you see how many colors there are in them. No cloud like this is ever pure white."

The instructor studied her reference photo a moment, then squeezed out a bit of blue, brown, and crimson paint. What odd color choices, I thought. Why did she not mix up some gray? Despite my uninformed skepticism, she created a cloud that reflected the light from her painted sky and the landscape beneath it. Her cloud cast shadows on itself and the green hills. Her cloud was realistic. Her cloud was shapely, buoyant, and bright. Her cloud looked settled and content—almost grateful to be the chosen cloud in a desired landscape.

The instructor had created this cloudscape seemingly effortlessly and in less than fifteen minutes. Impressed and perhaps a bit intimidated, the students moved slowly toward their own easels to try their hand at lifting clouds. Grateful at this moment to be a spectator, I thanked the instructor, waved a goodbye to the students, and moved toward the door.

"Here you go," the instructor said, handing me a large sheet of her expensive watercolor paper and copies of the two reference photos. "Why don't you try lifting some clouds at home."

How kind, I thought.

"You can join us next Monday to share what you create and to see what the other students have done."

How awful, I thought.

I had no talent for painting or interest in actually painting clouds. I had gotten what I came to the class for: an artist's perspective on clouds, a first-hand look at a cloud-painting technique, and a nice twist on the convective cycle. But it would have been awkward to refuse the instructor's generous offer, especially now, with the students looking over their easels and reading glasses at me as if to say, "We dare you."

I took the dare, took the paper, made my exit, and drove straight across town to the craft store. One hour and forty dollars later I had everything I needed to lift a cloud.

Taking advantage of the fair weather on this late spring day, I decided to work outside in the sun. At a big table on my back deck, I laid out my starter kit of watercolor paints, set of cheap brushes, a junior-size palette, glass jars for water, my watercolor paper, and a roll of paper towels. I didn't know how to start. So I sat down, shook out my arms, rolled my shoulders, flexed my fingers, took a deep breath, and picked up a brush.

Following my notes from class, I washed my paper with clear water and raw sienna, and then I dipped into the blues. I swept my brush back and forth across the top of the page, from edge to edge, diluting the paint as I moved down the paper. My French ultramarine did not fade gradually toward the horizon as in nature. It remained in bands—as in a Sherwin-Williams paint-sample card.

I wasn't too surprised at my results, to be honest. This was the way I did everything, proceeding forward merrily, blithely, to see what might happen, knowing I'd reach my goal eventually. Moving right along to the main event, I scrunched up a paper towel, pressed it smack-dab into the center of my sky, heard myself count "one Mississippi," and then picked up my hand. A white cloud!

Fueled by a surge of pride in Li'l Puffy, I quickly lifted a whole bunch more. Blot, blot, blot, blot, blot. Now there were six Li'l Puffy clouds floating at the same height and same distance apart all the way across my paper. I frowned. My clouds did not say, "Cumulus congestus coming soon." They said, "Sinking air crapping on thermals." My painting was jejune, cartoonish. It lacked convective conviction. It was so disappointing. Fortunately it was also close to dinnertime.

I left the painting there to dry and drove off to the grocery store a few miles away. When I emerged from the store some twenty minutes later, a bank of dark clouds had moved in from the southwest. When would I learn not to trust the weather in the Pacific Northwest? It had been sunny when I left home, and now big, fat raindrops splatted my windshield. When I got home, the sun was shining again. I set my grocery bags down on the kitchen table and looked out the window to my back deck. My heart sank.

The fat raindrops had left splash-craters in my striped blue sky and had blown out the soft, rounded edges of my white clouds. Irked, the real clouds had spat on my artificial ones. They had conspired against me to rebuke my truly mediocre Cumulus.

The silver lining? My watercolor paper had two sides.

Eventually I lifted some respectable billowy white clouds from a credibly homogeneous blue sky. When I tried to add color, however, I overworked my clouds into a deep-purple, toxic-looking mess. I was tempted to paint two industrial smokestacks beneath them. Instead I just lifted the dark colors out with a wet paper towel—and in the process inadvertently created a witch out of one cloud and added something resembling an elephant's trunk to the base of another.

I brought my painting to the Monday watercolor class.

The instructor approached me eagerly.

"Let's see!"

I handed her my homework.

"Oh—"

After an excruciatingly long pause, she added, "That's—not bad."

During the group critique, students took turns holding up their cloud paintings and describing what had gone right and wrong—mostly wrong. Even the more experienced painters said their clouds were "too large," "ponderous," "too dense," "bordering on psychedelic." Most of the students found that creating realistic-looking clouds was much more difficult than they expected.

"The harder you try, the worse they look."

"My cloud looks like it has indigestion."

"The clouds ruined my decent landscape."

"The more I look at it, the less I like it. It has a dragon face in it, and I'll never be able to look at it without seeing that."

"Clouds are too challenging."

"This looks like crap."

The instructor was sympathetic.

"When you start painting clouds," she said, "you start looking at clouds—really looking. Your relationship to them changes. That relationship becomes part of your painting."

I looked at my painting. My relationship with the clouds was definitely strange. I was happy to hear that, over time, this might change. I might one day paint a cloud that reflected my true feelings for them. Though they did not say so, the other students probably felt the same way.

The instructor offered several tips for improvement and then suggested that students use the rest of the class to finish their cloudscapes. When more than a few shoulders slumped, she added, "Or work on something else."

"I'm done with clouds," one student announced. Some students nodded in a mutinous way and then pulled out their unfinished paintings of barns and yellow warblers to work on.

Just as I was leaving, one student walked her worked-over cloud painting to the deep utility sink in the back of the classroom. She turned on the faucet, slid her half-finished cloud painting under the running water, and scrubbed it with a sponge as if it were a dirty cookie sheet. I didn't expect the paper to be so durable. Nor did I expect to feel a twinge of sadness as her diluted clouds flowed down the drain in a pale gray swirl.

Perhaps, I consoled myself, these rejected clouds would make their way down the plumbing pipes, over to the water treatment facility, and back into Puget Sound as pure water molecules. Perhaps they would skitter on the surface of the water in the sun and dance their way back into the sky on a rising thermal.

Cloud Ch'i

I called my mother-in-law, a talented landscape and still-life painter, to tell her about the watercolor class and my toxic, elephantine cloud.

"What I learned about clouds," she said, "I learned through Chinese brush-painting. Clouds have to have ch'i. Do you know what I mean by *ch'i*?"

"Energy?"

"Yes, but a certain kind of energy. It's the energy of life—in things that are living and not living. I'm going to send you something from *The Mustard Seed Catalog*."

"A seed catalog?"

"It's not a seed catalog. It's a Chinese painting manual. It's wonderful. It's old. Very old. I think it will help you with clouds."

A few days later, two photocopied pages from the manual arrived in the mail as promised. One page described the "*hsi kou* (small hook) outline style" of cloud painting and showed an example. The clouds were thick black lines that squirmed all down the page. They reminded me of a mermaid's long hair done in the wavy marcelled style popular in the 1920s. I could see the energy in the hook-like curves of the painted lines but not their resemblance to clouds.

The second page showed the *ta kou* (large hook) outline style. These clouds were looser, puffier, and more cloud-like but in no way resembled the clouds my mother-in-law—or any other Western artists I had studied—had painted in acrylic or oil.

When I requested *The Mustard Seed Catalog* from my public library, I found out that its actual title is *The Mustard Seed Garden Manual of Painting*. This still-popular manual of painting was created by three brothers, who were also painters, in Nanking, China, in 1679, and takes its name from the publisher of the book, who lived and worked nearby on a small property named the Mustard Seed Garden to indicate its smallness. My library copy was the 1887 "Shanghai edition" edited and reissued by Princeton University Press in 1978. It was 624 pages long and included four hundred examples of brushstroke forms and much wisdom.

This was not a how-to book about getting *ch'i* into clouds but a philosophical framework for painters based on the wisdom and perspective of "the ancients"—the painters, philosophers, literati, and authors of Confucian, Taoist, and Buddhist classics often quoted in the text. *The Mustard Seed Garden Manual of Painting* was not about what you were painting (clouds or any other subject) but how to think about your subject before you picked up your brush.

"Clouds are the ornaments of sky and earth," one passage begins, "the embroidery of mountains and streams. They may move as swiftly as horses. They may seem to strike a mountain with such force that one almost hears the sound of the impact. Such is the nature (*ch'i shih*, spirit and structural integration) of clouds."

Poetry or science? I wasn't sure, but it rang true, and I liked it.

"Among the ancients," the text states, "there were two key methods in painting clouds. First, in vast landscapes of numerous cliffs and valleys, clouds were used to divide (and to hide) parts of the scene. Richly verdant peaks soared into the sky and white scarves of clouds stretching horizontally separated and imprisoned them. Where the clouds parted, green summits rose. As the literati say: 'In the midst of hustling activity steal moments of quietness.'"

Steal moments of quietness? What an incongruous bit of advice, placed as it was, between the descriptions of the two methods of painting clouds.

"Second, in a landscape where mountains and valleys extend into the distance, clouds were used as a means of uniting them. The clouds sometimes filled spaces where there were no mountains or water, billowing like great waves of the ocean and soaring like mountain peaks."

I had experienced clouds hiding things (the sun, for example, and the landscape when it was foggy), but I had never thought of clouds as dividing, uniting, or filling parts of the landscape. The way I looked at them, clouds had a prepositional relationship with the landscape; clouds were above, below, behind, or in front of the mountains, trees, lake, and other scenery. How delightfully refreshing to learn that clouds had the capacity for a more active and intimate relationship with the landscape.

Not long after perusing *The Mustard Seed Garden Manual of Painting*, I caught the clouds and the landscape in flagrante delicto. It was the week before Christmas, and I was driving around town one afternoon in a frenzy of errands, including walking my old dog who had been patiently riding in the back of the car. We stopped at a newly graveled trail along the shore of Budd Inlet for what I hoped would be a brisk walk. My dog had another agenda—sniffing individual pieces of pea gravel every few feet. Rather than drag him along by his leash, I let him set the pace. This gave me ample time to stand still and study the scenery.

The tide was out, and the broad, tan mudflats were glistening and rippled—almost marcelled, like the small-hook clouds. A layer of fog—twenty feet thick or so—touched both western and eastern shores and covered the water as far as my eye could see. These clouds did indeed unite parts of the landscape. The soft firs, hemlocks, and cedars on the distant hills appeared and disappeared as the fog surged slowly over them.

Fifty miles to the northwest, a wide band of patchy clouds flirted with the Olympic Mountains, softly revealing and concealing their serrated, snow-covered peaks. As my dog sniffed, the late-afternoon light shifted. The soft gray fog darkened, the distant clouds turned cotton candy pink, and the white snow on the mountains glowed the ochre of a winter solstice sun. In the midst of hustling activity, I had stolen—no, had been given—this moment of quietness.

In *The Mustard Seed Garden Manual of Painting*, the discussion of clouds appears in a section called the "Book of Rocks." There is no "Book of Clouds" or "Book of Sky." An editorial note explains that "the ancients included

The similarities between clouds and rocks seems quite apparent in art and in nature—once you start looking.

clouds in their discussions of the main principles of painting mountains." Clouds were so integral to painting mountains that the ancients often called paintings of mountains "cloud-landscapes" and "cloud-water pictures."

The first page of the "Book of Rocks" features a brush painting of five rocks that could easily pass as five stylized Cumulus mediocris clouds. I had never thought of clouds as rock-like, but when I started looking at real clouds with rocks in mind, the similarities between the two were suddenly obvious. The sky became a geologic landscape where bold erratics, basin-and-range undulations, windswept dunes, and sedimentary layers of rock appeared in cloud form. What forces—wind? heat? atmospheric pressure? time?—could be working on rocks and clouds to create such similarities from such different raw material? An answer of sorts is included in the "Book of Rocks": "In estimating people, their quality of spirit (*ch'i*) is as basic as the way they are formed; and so it is with rocks, which are the framework of the heavens and of earth and also have *ch'i*. That is the reason rocks are sometimes spoken of as *yun ken* (roots of the clouds)."

I love this idea. Seeing rocks as the roots (*ken*) of clouds (*yun*) seems reasonable spiritually, aesthetically, and also meteorologically if you think of Cumulus clouds forming from thermals generated from sun-warmed rocks and boulders.

Rock-rooted clouds delight me for another reason. They allow me to invent a space—a just-plowed farm field stretching to the greening foothills of a snow-covered mountain peak. And they let me bend time to set into that landscape two men—one seventeenth-century Chinese brush painter, the other a fourteenth-century English farmer. I watch them as they stand side by side contemplating the clouds—the small Cumulus clouds I created for them. Neither man speaks a word, but they see the same things I see:

Rock.

Clod.

Root.

Ken.

Clûd.

Yun.

Cloud.

WATER

*A cloud is a visible mass of a **water** droplets or ice
crystals suspended in the atmosphere above the earth.*

When I think of water, I think first of the clear liquid I drink, swim in, and use for bathing and washing dishes. "Water," however, is not synonymous with "liquid water." Every day I forget this. It's easy to forget that water, H_2O, exists in three forms—liquid, solid, and vapor—at temperatures found naturally on Earth.

For most practical purposes here on Earth, "water" is synonymous with "water in its liquid phase." When we ask for a glass of water, we expect liquid water and not ice cubes. When we want ice cubes in our glass of water, we ask for "ice," not "solid water." When we talk about vapor (which we rarely do), we usually call it humidity (correct) or steam (wrong). Water vapor can also be called a gas. I prefer the term "vapor" because it doesn't make me think of gasoline, which—to confuse the issue—is a liquid I pump into my car.

A single molecule of water is made up of one atom of oxygen and two atoms of hydrogen. This molecule, H_2O, is the first one we learn about in school, often in early elementary school.

Water molecules are invisible, yet they appear in classrooms and textbooks around the world as three brightly colored balls or circles. One large ball or circle (usually red) represents one atom of oxygen; two smaller balls or circles (usually white) represent two atoms of hydrogen. Because of the way the hydrogen atoms bond to the oxygen atom—on the top and separated enough to look like two large ears on a head—the water molecule is often referred to as the "Mickey Mouse molecule."

Mickey Mouse, the balls, the circles—all of these are part of the conceptual model of a water molecule, an idea, a theory, a simplification, a convenience. The model is based on science, but it bears little resemblance to physical reality. There is no way to create a *physical* model—a scaled replica—of a water molecule. Models of microscopic particles and small things such as nematodes are scaled up for easier naked-eye viewing and study; models of large things such as whales and galaxies are scaled down for the same reasons. Scientists know that water is made of up of oxygen and hydrogen atoms at a one-to-two ratio, but no one has ever seen a single water molecule—not even with an atomic force microscope, which can show the atomic structure of other molecules. Water molecules are invisible to us not because water is "clear" or because the molecule is too small to see. It is invisible because a single water molecule is made up of atoms and those atoms are mostly empty space.

I was not fully prepared for the shock of this news when I read it in my chemistry textbook, though I was growing accustomed to the sudden twists and turns on my journey through the clouds. Rather than let the "little" fact about atoms derail my study of clouds and trigger a complete existential crisis, I did what every little kid does at Disney World: I clung to Mickey Mouse for dear life.

The Mickey Mouse model describes the relationship between the hydrogen and the oxygen atoms. Hydrogen atoms are separated by a 104.5° angle, with the positively charged particles (the protons) tending to be "clustered" at one end of the water molecule. This asymmetrical or unbalanced distribution of charge means that the hydrogen end of a water molecule has a positive charge, and the oxygen end a negative one. This makes H_2O a polarized molecule, also known as a dipole. Because of water's polarity, it is described as "sticky," which means it strongly attracts not only other water molecules but also other kinds of molecules. Not all molecules are polarized. Carbon dioxide, CO_2, for example, has one atom of carbon and two atoms of oxygen occurring on opposite sides of the carbon at 180°. If you think of water as Mickey Mouse, think of carbon as Princess Leia's hairdo in the *Star Wars* films.

The hydrogen atoms in water maintain their 104.5° separation from each other, but they are not bonded in a fixed position on the oxygen atom; they oscillate—moving from one side of the oxygen molecule to the other.

Visualize this as Mickey Mouse sliding his ears down to his chin and back to the top of his head constantly, rapidly, irritatingly.

At lower temperatures, most molecules shrink and become denser in solid form. Water does not. When water freezes into solid form, it expands and becomes lighter. This is why solid water (ice) floats on liquid water—in lakes, rivers, and a drinking glass.

In one DVD lecture I watched about water, the instructor discussed the structure of a water molecule while drawing it on a white board. When he was done, he turned, looked directly into the camera, and said, "Water is weird." The more I watched the clouds, the more I realized that they were weird too, and that the water molecule was likely the root cause. And I mean "weird" only in a good way—extravagantly strange, unpredictably varied, beautifully different, outright extraordinary.

Each of our ten cloud types may contain two or three forms of water simultaneously—vapor, water droplets, and ice crystals. The combination varies between the cloud types and changes over the lifetime of an individual cloud. So, in addition to thinking about the oscillating hydrogen atoms, I had to accept the fact that water molecules are moving fluidly between vapor, liquid, and solid phases. Change is occurring at the largest and smallest scales—from the overall mass of the cloud to atoms within it. Even clouds that seem stationary or slow-moving are in perpetual molecular turmoil. A cloud is a visible mass of invisible zinging, bouncing, jiggling, and darting. A cloud is a moon bounce, a pinball machine, a beehive, or a mosh pit of water. The clouds were becoming more dynamic than I expected.

The clouds became exhausting to watch. And when I wasn't looking at them, I was thinking about them. Even at night while I tried to sleep, I sensed they were always on, always moving, moving, moving, right over my roof. Was there no off switch for all this atmospheric water? Was there no still point in the clouds, some small particle or event—anything—I could focus on to let my weary mind rest?

Despite my restless sleep, I'd rally in the morning, step outside to get the paper and to greet the clouds, to let them know I'd been thinking about them all night.

Vapor

Vapor is the most abundant form of water in the atmosphere and is present in and at the edges of every type of cloud. If you are like me, the word "vapor" conjures up images of the white, misty, smoke-like substance rising from a steam plant or teakettle. This is not vapor. This is steam. Steam is created when liquid water is heated to boiling point, evaporates, and then quickly condenses into tiny droplets of visible liquid water. Vapor is different. Vapor is not a liquid, and it is not visible. Vapor is an invisible gas. Yet even when I think "invisible vapor," I see a patch of fumes floating nebulously in the blue sky. I do not see nothing. And I'm not the only one.

An internet image search of "water vapor" yielded me nearly two million images of clouds, snow, steam rising from power plants and teakettles, very visible oceans, and water-cycle maps. When I narrowed the search to "invisible water vapor," the image bank shrank only slightly. For fun, I did an image search on "invisible" and then spent the next ten minutes scanning through hundreds of images—mostly of people's clothes standing around with no one inside them, variations of Renee Magritte's painting *The Son of Man* minus the green apple and man's face, scenes with certain objects cropped out, and cats in midair poses that made them appear to be riding invisible motorcycles.

When I say water vapor is invisible, I mean invisible to the naked eye. We can use technology to see water vapor thanks to the Geostationary Operational Environment Satellite (GOES) system. This system detects water vapor in the atmosphere from 22,300 miles above the earth. The satellites are launched by the National Aeronautics and Space Administration (NASA) and operated by the National Oceanic and Atmospheric Administration (NOAA). NOAA, NASA, and the National Weather Service (NWS) all use the imagery for scientific research and weather monitoring and forecasting. In the still images, vapor appears as beautiful, sinuous, cloud-like swirls.

Although we cannot see water vapor with the naked eye, we can sense it with our naked skin. Only we don't call it vapor. We call it humidity. Humidity is the measure of the amount of water vapor in the air.

As a child growing up in the very muggy Washington, DC, area, I believed that the weather report of "98 percent relative humidity" meant that the air would turn liquid when it reached 100 percent, which was *any minute now.* I was so grateful for that 2 percent of "dry" air that saved me, my dog, and everyone I knew from drowning in a liquid sky when we inhaled. I never thought to ask, "98 percent of what?"

Turns out it's 98 percent of almost nothing.

"Relative humidity" describes the relationship between the maximum amount of water vapor that *could be* in a parcel of air and the amount of water vapor that is actually in that parcel under the atmospheric conditions at the time it is measured. The amount of water vapor varies over time, under different atmospheric conditions, and from place to place. In colder Arctic areas it can be a fraction of a percent. In hot, tropical jungles, it can be as high as 4 percent.

If, for example, a parcel of air could contain 4 percent of its volume in water vapor but actually only contains 1 percent, the relative humidity is 25 percent; that is, the air contains a quarter of the water vapor it could. Later that day, as atmospheric conditions change, humidity might increase to 3 percent, and the relative humidity would then be 75 percent, the air containing three-quarters of the vapor it could. When our air parcel contains the maximum amount of water vapor possible under current conditions, 4 percent in this case, the relative humidity is 100 percent. At this point, the parcel of air is considered "saturated." At this point, if our saturated air is sufficiently cooled, a cloud will begin to form and rain may follow. Not even at 100 percent will we find ourselves underwater, drowning in water vapor.

Mickey Mouse

After one particularly long day of studying the water molecule, I had reached my mental saturation point. I turned off my computer and went for a long walk and didn't look up. I knew the clouds would be up there, merrily floating while I struggled miserably on their behalf.

When I returned home, I played a CD of Chopin's piano music in an attempt to drive the swirling clouds and busy water molecules from my mind. It was no use. I fixed dinner then got in my car and headed downtown for an evening class. At a traffic light I pulled up behind a gray car. The light was long and I had time to notice the name of the car—STRATUS—spelled in big silver letters across the trunk.

I stared at the letters, amused that the marketing staff at Dodge must have thought "Stratus" sounded important and lofty like "status" or "stratosphere," which it does if you don't know your clouds.

Just below the S in "Stratus," there was a bright green Mickey Mouse decal in a running posture surrounded by four brightly colored Mickey Mouse symbols. Water molecules!

There I was, staring at a full-body Mickey chasing four water molecules on a fog-gray Stratus. Mere coincidence? A joke from the cosmos? A writer losing her grip?

I needed a water break.

The next morning, I turned my attention to a more stable ingredient in a cloud.

Particles

Even our cleanest air contains microscopic solid particles—salt, pollen, plant spores, phytoplankton, microbes, bacteria, viruses, soot, clay, sulfates, nitrates, and myriad other minerals and chemical compounds. These particles are often called "dirt" or "dust," but scientists prefer to call them "particles," "particulate matter," or "aerosols" (a word combining Greek *aero*, meaning "air," and a shortened form of "solids"). I'll compromise and use "particles."

Some of these particles enter the atmosphere naturally through ocean spray, volcanic eruptions, forest wildfires, dust storms, gasses emitted from plants, and updrafts. Others are introduced through human activity, including the burning of fossil fuels, manufacturing, slash-and-burn agricultural fires, and soil disturbance caused by construction, mining, and farming. While some particles linger in the lower atmosphere near their source, many rise into the upper atmosphere and travel the globe, often moving in vast swirls and eddies.

These invisible particles range in size from 0.002 micrometers to 20 micrometers in diameter. The size most important for cloud formation falls between 0.2 and 2.0 micrometers. There are thousands to hundreds of thousands of such particles floating in every square inch of air.

Imagine a parcel of invisible warm air containing billions of these tiny particles rising on a thermal. As the water vapor in that parcel cools, the individual water vapor molecules slow down and more readily cling to each other and condense on the surface of these floating particles, which are known as condensation nuclei. These nuclei are tiny but commodious. When at least a billion water vapor molecules have gathered on a condensation nucleus, the vapor changes phase and becomes visible liquid water—a cloud droplet. Billions upon billions of these cloud droplets—each with a tiny particle at their center—make up a cloud.

The size and concentration of cloud-condensation nuclei in our atmosphere affect the size, quantity, and—increasingly—the appearance and function of the clouds. Some nuclei, especially those produced through the combustion of fossil fuels, can increase the quantity of cloud droplets but decrease their size. This causes more sunlight to be reflected back into space, thus darkening the clouds at their bases. Clouds forming around these small nuclei may increase the overall cooling of the planet. Scientists have not yet determined if the cooling effect of these clouds might counterbalance the warming effect of the water, carbon dioxide, methane, nitrous oxide, and other heat-trapping greenhouse gasses.

The water vapor molecules in our atmosphere are discriminating in their choice of condensation nuclei but only to a point. They cannot resist condensing around particles we might prefer they didn't. Liquid cloud droplets cannot resist developing into clouds that will rain these toxins on the land and water—ours and our downwind neighbors' across the globe. In the 1850s, for example, a scientist discovered that cloud droplets that condensed on nitrogen oxides and sulfur dioxides generated through combustion had higher acidity levels than normal raindrops. It was not until the 1960s that scientists began studying the damaging effects of "acid rain"—and also acid fog, acid snow, and acid hail—on plants and wildlife, especially fish and aquatic insects.

We cannot blame the clouds for these problems. They are just doing their job, following the laws of physics, playing their critical role in the water cycle. We are to blame. We should be more discriminating in the ingredients we offer the sky.

Altocumulus

For a long while, Altocumulus clouds remained on my "to do later" list because they were the most challenging of the ten cloud genera to identify. In the Pacific Northwest, these mid-level clouds are often blocked from view by lower cloud layers so when they did appear—in one of four possible species and seven varieties—they frustrated me. I did not want a love-hate relationship with the clouds but a love-love one. So I ignored Altocumulus clouds until I was ready for them. I recommend this strategy for any cloud that gives you trouble.

Altocumulus clouds occur between 6,500 and 23,000 feet above the earth. They can appear as layers, rounded masses, or rolls and be white, gray, or a combination of the two. Altocumulus are relatively thin water-droplet clouds. Because they have "cumulus" as part of their name, I assumed that Altocumulus formed by convection, but these clouds are too high for thermals to reach. There are, however, pockets and layers of rising and falling air aloft in the atmosphere, and Altocumulus clouds are a response to this air. These clouds also form from dissipating layers of Altostratus, and they are a welcome sight after a long siege of horizon-to-horizon gray.

When Altocumulus appear as rounded masses or rolls, they can be difficult to differentiate from higher Cirrocumulus and lower Stratocumulus. A handy way to tell them apart is to hold your hand at arm's length so your stacked fingers (held together, not spread apart) cover one of the individual elements (a cloudlet). If your cloudlet is between one and three fingers wide, you are looking at an Altocumulus. Less than one finger of width means you are looking at a Cirrocumulus, more than three fingers means a Stratocumulus.

No skill or practice is needed to spot an Altocumulus lenticularis—the distinctively smooth, lens-shaped clouds often mistaken for UFOs because they hover like enormous flying saucers over mountainous landscapes. These clouds are eye-catching, photogenic, and so common that they have a nickname—"lennies."

Lennies can appear singly or in multiples. They can line up horizontally or stack themselves vertically like dinner plates or pancakes on the leeward side of a mountain barrier. In midday light, lennies are bright white and often strongly shaded at their base or along one side. At sunset, they take on pastel orange and pink hues and a surreal look.

These clouds are not endemic to Washington, but when they float just downwind of Mount Rainier or other snowcapped volcanic peaks in the Cascade Range, they attain the rank of salmon, orca whales, and the Space Needle as icons of the state. I must confess, though, lennies left me cold at first. Images of these clouds appear all too often on postcards and wall calendars and to decorate tourist tchotchkes. They seemed a bit too popular, even bordering on commercial. I warmed up to them when I learned how they form.

Lennies form when moist air in the mid-altitude range encounters a mountain peak and begins to rise. As it rises on the windward side, it reaches its condensation level and forms a cloud. Lennies do not continue to rise into the atmosphere like Cumulus clouds because lennies form in stable air, which returns to its original level after being forced to rise. Cumulus clouds, on the other hand, form in unstable air—air that does not return to its original position after being forced to rise.

After lennies rise and form, therefore, they descend on the leeward side of the mountain, trying to return to their original altitude. As they sink, the air temperature warms and the liquid water droplets in the cloud evaporate. Often, the rising and sinking pattern of the air established by the mountain continues for some distance downwind in its lee. Lennies may form in the crest of each leeward wave until the wave settles to below condensation level.

The Cap Cloud

Of all the clouds I have seen atop Mount Rainier, the one I remember best and recall most often looked like a cap. What made this cloud so memorable was not its shape but its appearance out of the blue on the right day, in the right place, and in the right company.

One August morning in Olympia, the air was bright and clear, and the glossy-needled firs, hemlocks, and cedars shimmered and sparkled. The sun had been at work a few hours already, warming the earth and nudging the cool air toward the predicted and exquisite 77°F.

There were no clouds in the sky on this perfect day—no threat of them and no opacity of light that might betray a nascent one. There was just pure, unimpeded sunlight that glorified everything it illuminated—leaves, boughs, bark, skin, edges of things, and, sitting across from me on my back porch that morning, my father.

He had just arrived the night before from the East Coast for his first trip without my mother, his cherished wife of fifty-four years, who had died that June from a heart attack. Just two months ago my father and I were dressed in black and reading eulogies. Now we were in jeans, reading maps. My father and I were planning our trip to Paradise.

Paradise was just 5,400 feet above us and perched on the southern flank of Mount Rainier. The area known as Paradise offers visitors to Mount Rainier National Park plenty of parking, a visitors' center, a historic inn, hiking trails to waterfalls and alpine meadows, routes to the icy summit, and panoramic views too broad and deep for any camera to capture. Paradise was a long but easy day trip from Olympia. My father and I set out after breakfast for a creaky-knees stroll and lunch at the Paradise Inn.

This was our first trip together, just the two of us. My father has always been a strong "can-do" man with action plans and the willpower to execute them. But this day, deeply affected by his recent loss, he seemed sapped of his strength. He was more passive than he'd ever been, more content to sit and listen to the conversations around him rather than to participate in his usual engaging and jocular style.

A few miles south on Interstate 5, it became apparent my mother had been the one who had driven our conversations. Without her questions and often-funny remarks, there was a lot of silence. I felt the need to be entertaining and so I began a tour-guide spiel, naming the rivers we crossed, the towns we bypassed, the Cascade peaks north and south of Mount Rainier.

Nothing I said required a response or elicited a comment.

It was time to change gears, to acknowledge that talking about my mother was not off-limits, to let my father know it was okay to be sad and grieve even if our day trip had the trappings of a fun vacation.

"It must be strange traveling without Mom," I said.

"It's all strange," my father replied.

I waited for more, but that was it.

I let the silence in.

He was right. It was all strange: the way my mother's eighty-six years had ended just three weeks after her heart attack, the way two months had passed already but too slowly since her death, the way my mother's presence was palpable despite her absence, and my father's sudden and unexpected solitude. Just contemplating this made my heart clench. I was relieved that my father hadn't articulated what he meant by "strange." It would have been too much. So we kept on—me pointing out big trees and glimpses of Mount Rainier, my father looking and listening. Eventually he tilted his seat back and announced he was going to take a short nap.

He was snoring within minutes. I was glad. Asleep, he wouldn't have to listen to my tedious monologue or imagine seeing my mother in his peripheral vision, sitting in the back seat of the car, ready with a wink or remark to make him laugh.

My father woke as I pulled off at Ricksecker Point for a leg stretch and our first big view of the mountain. This close—just six miles south of the summit as the crow flies—Mount Rainier appeared as a rugged, horizon-dominating mass of dark and jagged rock, snowfields, and glaciers flowing from the summit like thick slices of melted white cheese. Through our binoculars, the glaciers were nothing like cheese but instead a rough jumble of massive irregularly shaped blocks of ice separated by crevasses—deep wedge-shaped spaces that trapped blue light the color of the Caribbean.

Just as I was about to stop looking, something caught my eye: a pale smudge of a cloud floating directly over the mountain. Narrow bands of cloud radiated from it like an airbrushed sunburst. The surrounding skies were still deep blue and cloudless. Given the summit's height of 14,411 feet, I figured the smudge was a mid-level cloud, although it didn't look like any Altocumulus or Altostratus I had ever seen. It looked more like fog or smoke coming off the glaciers. I photographed the cloud—and then my father in front of the mountain—and we resumed our drive.

Though the entrance road and the parking lot at Paradise were snow-free, all the trails on the mountain were still under snow—nearly four feet of it, according to the first ranger we asked. On this warm and sunny August day, Paradise was no place for us sneaker-clad day-trippers seeking wildflowers. It was a winter wonderland for snowshoers, crampon-equipped hikers, and kids on snow saucers.

We took in the views from the parking lot, ate lunch, and then wandered down to the visitors' center for a little while. On this day, we both wanted to be outside in the bright sun to see what was happening on the mountain.

What was happening was a cloud.

The smudge of cloud we had seen from Ricksecker Point had developed into a soft-spun whiteness that now enveloped the summit like a floppy wool cap. I wondered if it was a lennie in the making and told my father all about them. I so wanted this cloud to rise off the summit while we were watching it, to rise and take off like a spaceship.

My father and I stood in the sun, listening to the trickle of melting snow all around us, and watched the cloud. This cloud did not develop into a lennie. It did not rise or change shape. This cloud didn't budge. It just hugged the summit protectively.

According to one of my cloud guides, we were looking at a cap cloud. A cap cloud is not one of the official cloud species or varieties, according to the World Meteorological Organization, but a supplementary feature known as a pileus, which forms on top of Cumulus and Cumulonimbus clouds—and also atop mountain peaks. Unlike lennies and other Altocumulus clouds, cap clouds form as light winds near the surface of the ground move warm air horizontally. A cap cloud exists in a state of balanced flux—condensing on the windward side of the summit and evaporating at the same rate on the leeward side. Such a strange cloud. There it was, created from the usual turmoil of water molecules but now resting in apparent equilibrium atop a formidable, unpredictable mountain.

My father and I took turns looking through my binoculars at our cap cloud. Neither of us could detect any movement at its edges or smooth top. I wanted this mountain to make my father strong. I wanted this air to bring him stability, this cloud to bring him equilibrium—for him to take pleasure in the increased attention of family and friends gathering on the windward side, and to be at peace with the loss of my mother's love in the lee.

After a while, we strolled back to the car and drove down the mountain, slowing to admire the wildflowers blooming along the roadside at lower elevations. As lovely as the sun-splashed patches of bright lupine, hellebore, paintbrush, and lilies were, they paled in comparison to the cloud from Paradise.

My father didn't say much on the drive back home, but I sensed that he loved that mountain and the cloud as much as he possibly could that day. After he returned home, he sent me a note thanking me for a "splendid visit" and for the booklet of photographs I had sent him of our trip. "The prize," he wrote, "was Mt. Rainier and the Cap Cloud. At that distance it looked almost religious—immutable, immovable, impregnable, ageless and even comforting."

Glory

The October following my father's visit, I flew back to Virginia for the first time since my mother's death. Since moving west a decade earlier, I'd been flying across the country a few times a year—usually with my husband and two sons, but now that my sons were in college, I made more frequent solo trips. Not until my eastbound plane rose through the low, gray Stratus over Seattle did it hit me: my mother was not going to be there at the end of this long flight. The old farmhouse I grew up in—the house my parents lived in and loved for forty years—would still look the same, but it would be empty. Not de-cluttered but empty. Empty in a way I had never known. The very thought of this filled me with sadness and dread.

I turned my shoulders toward the window, stared down onto the sea of lumpy gray clouds, and began to cry. It was not the brief downpour I had hoped for. I mopped my eyes with one of my mother's white monogrammed handkerchiefs. I tried not to whimper or sob. I sniffled a lot and kept my gaze on the clouds to distract myself. The clouds thinned as we crossed the Cascade Mountains. Between the patches of clouds, I could see green and golden farmland and then stretches of the Columbia River. I wished my mother could have seen how beautiful the earth looked through the clouds.

She had taken great pleasure in my interest in clouds. Early on, she sent me postcards of clouds, newspaper clippings about clouds, and a book of photographs called *Extraordinary Clouds*. She put sticky notes on the pages featuring her favorites: "I like Cirrus castellanus!" "Wheeee! Cirrus plumes are upbeat!" "Cirrus uncinus look like angels." Though she had lost her interest in flying in recent years, my mother would have marveled at the clouds I was looking at now and at the very strange sight that appeared out my window as we reached 30,000 feet.

Below the plane and just behind the wing, a tiny, faint shadow of our airplane appeared on the thick layer of Altocumulus cloud. Encircling the shadow were rings of light—like a rainbow-colored halo, only more diffuse. As our plane's shadow moved across the clouds, the circles of light moved with it as if escorting us.

Were my tears and the sunlight playing tricks on me? I dried my eyes and took out my glasses. The tiny shadow sharpened. The circle of light held the plane in its center. Both moved across the clouds. It was beautiful, even comforting.

I plucked a paperback book out of my purse—*Science from Your Airplane Window*—an out-of-print treasure and gift from my oldest son. Inside the front cover were two color photographs. One looked exactly like what I was seeing out my window. "The glory from a seat just behind the wing," the caption read.

A glory is not a cloud but one of the many rainbow-like optical phenomena associated with clouds. Glories appear in clouds composed of water droplets, such as the Altocumulus we were flying over. To create a glory, the sunlight does a very strange U-turn inside the cloud droplets. As the sunlight enters the cloud droplet, it is refracted toward the back of the droplet, where it is then reflected before being diffracted again. This diffraction separates the light into separate wavelengths that exit the cloud droplet and head back

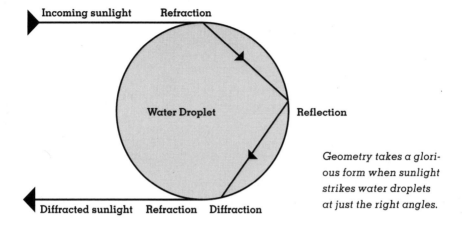

Geometry takes a glorious form when sunlight strikes water droplets at just the right angles.

toward its source—the sun—with you there in the very center of its path seeing the rings of color—the glory—in the cloud.

Compared to a rainbow, a glory is small, subtle, and easy to miss. If you are in a window seat, you can increase your chances of seeing a glory by looking out and scanning the clouds as if you are searching for something you have lost.

Had I had the chance to see a glory with my mother, I would not have told her how they formed. She was a poet and preferred her natural wonders to be left uncomplicated by science. She loved to be in awe and to remain there as long as she could. When I first told her that the "evening star" she frequently pointed out was actually a planet, she gave me a look and said, "I'm calling it a star."

I find little comfort in imagining my mother in a heaven where the dearly departed float and mingle in the clouds for eternity. But after seeing that glory, I felt an unexpected solace knowing that—every once in a while—a cloud might hold me and my mother together in an embrace—me in a shadow, she in the rings of light.

Meteorologists may call it a glory.

I'm calling it Mom.

DROPLETS

*A cloud is a visible mass of water **droplets** or ice crystals suspended in the atmosphere above the earth.*

First things first: cloud droplets are not teardrop-shaped. They are tiny, spherical balls or globes. Raindrops are not teardrop-shaped either. Small raindrops are spherical, and large ones are shaped like hamburger buns—flat on the bottom and slightly convex on the top. Even human tears are not teardrop shaped. When they appear (in eyes and on cheeks) they are shaped like puddles and rivers. The only time water droplets naturally assume the teardrop shape is when, as a collection of *many* droplets, they drip from a leaky faucet.

The teardrop shape we have come to associate with "drops" and "droplets" is artifice—a symbol, a pop-culture icon, an artifact of bad science. Though scientists at the United States Geologic Survey (USGS) surely know better, their public education staff relies on the friendly, teardrop-shaped icon known as "Drippy" to help educate the public on the shape of raindrops. One educator-entrepreneur has made a cottage industry out of the water cycle using a similarly pointy-headed droplet he calls "Mr. Drippy" to adorn the teaching materials he sells.

Marketing aside, cloud droplets are round. They measure between 2 and 200 micrometers in diameter. Inside any cloud, the droplets exist in many different sizes, and each droplet changes size frequently during its time in the cloud as it condenses and evaporates. When droplets grow to between 200 and 500 micrometers, they are called "drizzle drops" or simply "drizzle" because they are of sufficient size to fall (drop) out of the cloud. Drizzle doesn't fall hard or fast until it exceeds 500 micrometers and is then classified as raindrops.

The Dance of Sunlight and Water

Cloud droplets are visible because they are large enough to scatter white light equally and become part of a visible white cloud. What was really going on inside the droplets, I wondered, that enabled them to scatter sunlight this way? If, as my husband and Isaac Newton suggested, the visible-spectrum wavelengths in sunlight were simply bouncing off the surface of a cloud droplet and not penetrating it, why would it matter to wavelengths whether they were bouncing off a 2-micrometer-wide cloud droplet or a 500-micrometer-wide raindrop? If the wavelengths did penetrate the cloud droplet, was it the size of the droplet or the billions of water molecules in the droplet that mattered? The answer was not to be found anywhere in my growing collection of science books.

Knowing what the internet might do with any search containing the words "size" and "matters," I typed in this ridiculously long phrase: "Do individual wavelengths of visible light enter the molecules of water within a cloud droplet or do they bounce off its surface before they are scattered?" This excluded not only Viagra ads but also any scholarly article comprehendible to the unscholarly reader. Where to turn?

I reached out to the Outreach Program at the University of Washington's (UW) Department of Atmospheric Sciences in Seattle. If the team of graduate student volunteers who ran this program could, as their website indicated, explain weather and meteorology to hundreds of school groups—kindergarteners through twelfth-graders—surely they could explain the secret of a cloud droplet to me.

Less than twenty-four hours after my email request, I got a reply from the outreach coordinator himself. After a few rounds of pesky questions (from me) and generous responses (from him), I had a primer on geometric-optics scattering, Rayleigh scattering, Mie scattering, multiple scattering, Maxwell's equations, and a succinct explanation of why clouds are white according to the laws of classical physics.

"Remember," he wrote, "even at 2 micrometers, a cloud droplet is much larger than the wavelengths of visible sunlight, which are between 0.4 and 0.7 micrometers. The scattering is mostly a result of the individual particles of light—the photons—*refracting* (slightly changing direction) every time they encounter the *surface* of one of the water droplets or ice crystals, whether 'diving' into it or emerging from it!"

The bold-faced type was his. I liked his enthusiasm.

"The droplets or ice bits are much bigger than the photons, so the photons just see them as an ordinary volume of water or ice—like an ice cube or the surface of a pond. The photons sail along through the air, encounter the water (or ice) surface, change directions a bit as they break into the droplet or crystal, plow straight along through the interior of the droplet or crystal in the new direction, until they hit the other side, refract again as they emerge back out into the air and sail off in this newest direction."

The idea of invisible photons seeing, sailing, breaking in, plowing, and sailing off again made me happy.

"Refraction is the 'the big kahuna' in the clouds though sometimes the photons are also reflected back in the direction they came. Then they encounter another cloud droplet and are refracted again and again. With all of this refraction and reflection going on—and on and on—as the photons make their way through the mass of water droplets in the cloud, the photons in each wavelength are thoroughly scattered."

When I asked him what the photons were really doing down in the cloud droplet to make the light scatter this way or that, he said I needed a physicist.

Before I took him up on his offer, I read articles on atmospheric optics, light absorption, and theories about the interactions of light and matter. I dipped my toes into physics and its subfields—quantum mechanics and quantum electrodynamics, or QED. I understood that "quantum" was simply a name for discrete units of energy—electrons, protons, neutrons, and photons—and that this "quantized matter" was interacting all the time everywhere in theoretically predictable but uncertain ways. I had a hunch that the answer to my question was in one of the strings of numbers, symbols, and both Greek and Roman alphabet letters that appeared in scientific articles. I was over my head, and not even Richard Feynman—Nobel Prize–winning physicist, teacher, and author of very entertaining and accessible books and essays on QED—could explain the clouds to an English major like me. There was a big difference between QED and the OED, though a person could drown in either.

Eventually I found my way to the outreach coordinator's office at the UW. On his desk was a large glass jar full of clear glass marbles.

"I thought you'd like to see this," he said. "Think of a cloud as being like collections of zillions of tiny, floating pieces of colorless glass. Clouds will appear to be whatever color is illuminating them. If sunlight shines on them (as usual), they scatter white light back to us. If sunsets aim red light at them, they appear pink or red. If they are shadowed, they may appear gray."

I looked at the marbles. They were clear, more or less.

"When I shine a white light on them," he said, as he shone a flashlight on them, "they are white."

Sure enough. The marbles looked more white than clear. This demonstration made it seem so simple—too simple, perhaps. Glass marbles appeared to behave like cloud droplets, but silica was not water, and I wasn't convinced they scattered white light for same reasons.

The outreach coordinator then introduced me to one of his colleagues, a physics major working on a graduate degree in atmospheric sciences, someone who knew about clouds and their subatomic lives and had agreed to a conversation about cloud droplets and the whiteness of clouds.

I flatter myself to call what happened between me and this brilliant young man a conversation. For an hour he talked and I mostly said things like "uh-huh, uh-huh," "wow," and "hmmmm." We were sitting in a small conference room facing a huge whiteboard. I told him about all the dead ends I had reached trying to find my way into a cloud droplet.

"The explanations of what's going on in the atmosphere can certainly be confusing," he began, "because people like me who've studied quantum mechanics at the graduate level rarely become atmospheric scientists, while atmospheric scientists all learn non-quantum-mechanical-based explanations of phenomenon because they're not physicists."

I was thrilled to think my garden-variety confusion could be attributed to an internecine disconnect among scientists.

He drew a few Ns and Os on the whiteboard—the atmosphere of nitrogen and oxygen. He drew a classic Mickey Mouse—the water molecule. A few squiggly lines—sunlight. And then a stick figure in the middle of it all—the human observer of the magic of light and water.

"The hydrogen and oxygen atoms are mostly empty space," he began. "They each contain a nucleus of protons and neutrons. The nucleus is surrounded by electrons, which occupy a kind of cloud-shaped space."

A cloud-shaped space—fun! There I was inside a cloud, inside a droplet, inside a water molecule, inside an atom, and then in another cloud.

He sat down in his chair, staring pensively at his drawing.

"At this point—where the sunlight reaches the cloud—it is easier if you change the way you treat the light."

I was all for making this easier.

"Rather than treat sunlight as a wave," he said, "imagine it as photons. These photons are like electrons in that they are particles that behave like waves, but photons come from sunlight. As you lie on a sunny beach, there are 10^{20} photons hitting you per second."

The way he said it, I knew this was a lot of photons.

"Wow."

The number "ten to the twentieth," I learned later, is also expressed as "one hundred quintillion." It looks much larger when you write it out as the number "10" followed by twenty zeros: 1,000,000,000,000,000,000,000.

"When the sunlight reaches a cloud," he continued, "the photons get absorbed and reemitted by the electrons *somewhere* within the hydrogen and oxygen atoms."

"Where are the electrons when the sunlight hits the cloud droplet?" I asked.

"In this space, the electrons zing around so randomly," he said, "that scientists can only offer probabilities of their position in the atom at any given time."

"Why can't they figure out where it is?" I asked.

"It's not that physics is lacking something or that our understanding isn't complete. The electron simply has no definite position. It's like asking where, precisely, an ocean wave is. It's not really in one place but it's smeared out over a range of places. All we can talk about are the probabilities of finding the electron in certain types of locations around the nucleus."

"An electron absorbs a photon and reemits a photon," he continued. "There is no bouncing of photons off the surfaces of the water molecules. There is only absorbing and reemitting by the electrons in the atoms."

Which, I wanted to joke, might look like bouncing if you blink.

"When the sun shines white light on clouds, a photon might encounter an electron or it might not."

I wanted more certainty. I was desperate to find that one infinitesimally small moment or place in a cloud droplet where the thing that made a cloud white happened. I wanted the subatomic equivalent of a gate latch, train-car coupling, a high-five hand slap. I explained this to him.

He shrugged his shoulders.

"Uncertainty is simply built into the nature of the universe we inhabit."

I thought this was a no, but just to be sure I asked, "So, no one can isolate a fixed point or precise moment when an electron absorbs or reemits the photon inside the atoms in a water droplet?"

"No."

That was a no. I accepted this. I believe this young physicist would have told me if he had known.

"Clouds are composed of a complex mixture of droplets of all different sizes," he said. "The configuration of these droplets with air in between makes the scattering probabilities very complex. If there are enough cloud droplets, no direction of photon emission will be preferred."

I must have looked like I needed a metaphor.

"If I shine white light on a sheet of normal glass, 96 percent of the photons are going to be absorbed and remitted in such a way that they will appear to go straight through the glass; 4 percent of the photons are reflected back to our eyes. If I take that same sheet of glass and crush it up into millions of pieces, I've completely changed the probabilities into a much more complex situation in which no direction will be favored over another."

"And you get whiteness like the glass marbles in the jar?" I asked.

"Same idea. When the sun shines white light on clouds they, by nature of their chemical structure and physical configuration, absorb and reemit lots of photons in many directions, making them appear white to people on land, in the sky, and in space."

"Why do most explanations of a cloud's whiteness use the term 'scattering' instead of 'absorb and reemit'?" I asked.

"Fundamentally the only process going on is absorption and emission of photons by electrons. 'Scattering' is just a different word historically used in non-quantum explanations of the phenomena. Scattering is usually considered a 'bulk phenomenon,' and professional meteorologists don't need to know what is happening at the subatomic level to understand what is happening with the clouds or weather."

I understood his point. Judging by the way my head was spinning after just an hour inside the atom, I might not have noticed if the Atmospheric Sciences building had been swept up in a tornado. I thanked the physicist for his time, took a few photographs of the whiteboard, and closed my notebook.

"Don't be discouraged," he said before I left. "Physics is hard and takes time to absorb, but once it's absorbed the results can be very beautiful and powerful."

I wanted to absorb it all on my drive back to Olympia, but the subatomic life of a cloud seemed less and less relevant to the visibility and the whiteness of clouds. I imagined the absurdity of a subatomic weather forecast with a meteorologist standing in front of the TV cameras, pointing to satellite maps, and simply shrugging with uncertainty. I had zoomed in too far on the clouds. A person can explain how to build a birdhouse without knowing how the electrons in the carbon molecules in the wood interact with the electrons in the iron molecules in the nails. Those interactions are undoubtedly happening; they just don't help explain how a nail can hold two pieces of wood together.

In the weeks following my visit to the Department of Atmospheric Sciences, I began reading *Clouds in a Glass of Beer: Simple Experiments in Atmospheric Physics*—a book the outreach director had recommended. This marvelous book by Craig F. Bohren, a physicist and distinguished professor emeritus of meteorology at Pennsylvania State University, included a chapter entitled "Multiple Scattering at the Breakfast Table," which offered a different approach to understanding why clouds were white.

Bohren asks his readers to observe a shaker of salt and a bowl of sugar and to note that it's not something *in* these white particles that makes them white when light shines on them, but that the particles are so abundant. Cloud droplets, like particles of salt and sugar, do not absorb much light. Individually, these particles scatter light preferentially. Preferential scattering, recall, means that certain wavelengths in the visible spectrum are scattered more than others. Collectively, however, all of these particles scatter all wavelengths non-preferentially, or equally, to give us the color white.

This seemed to echo the glass marbles in the jar demonstration, but I wasn't sure. Did salt and sugar behave like water? I sent Dr. Bohren an email just in case things had gotten more complicated in the thirty years since his book was published. I presented my problem: understanding what was really going on inside a cloud droplet as it scattered sunlight. He replied almost immediately.

"You will be told clouds are white because cloud droplets are much larger than the wavelengths of visible sunlight, that they are nonselective scatterers. The nonselective part is true but it is a sufficient—not a necessary—condition. Clouds are usually white because they are thick."

By thick, Bohren means optically thick. This is not the same as physically thick. A cloud is considered optically thick when a high concentration of scatterers (the water droplets) shortens the average straight distance light can travel before it changes direction. In other words, in an optically thick cloud, the incoming photons don't get very far before they scatter. This optical thickness is the bigger player in the whiteness of clouds.

"Sugar in a bowl is white," says Bohren. "So is a bag of flour. So is snow. So is powdered glass. So are clouds. The list is long. The only commonality is that the absorption of visible wavelengths by these particles is negligible and that there are lots of particles. If you look at a single cloud droplet (sugar crystal, flour grain, glass shard, etc.), you would most likely call it transparent."

Was there a way I could explain why small nitrogen or oxygen molecules in the atmosphere scattered blue light and larger cloud droplets scattered all the wavelengths equally?

"Explaining why small particles are selective scatterers," he wrote, "whereas particles the size of a cloud droplet are not—in such a way that the general readers will understand—is essentially impossible."

Was there a way to use QED to explain this? (I was really reaching here.)

"If you are an optical physicist," he wrote, "charged with designing a multilayer interference filter, 'in principle' you use QED, but don't try if you want to keep your job or avoid being confined to an insane asylum."

Right.

And furthermore:

"To really understand light and color you need to know physics, physiology, and psychology. Without some understanding of all three, you are likely to completely misunderstand what humans perceive."

I took Dr. Bohren's point, though it pained me to have the door closed so firmly on my quest. I knew my limits. I hoped the clouds forgave me for failing to understand the inner workings of their inscrutable little droplet-shaped hearts.

Drop It

My husband had been on a long business trip during my crash course in physics. The evening he returned, we sat down in front of the fireplace in our living room with a glass of wine. I wanted to hear about his trip but not before I debriefed him on what I had learned about the cloud droplet. Despite the fact that he had just crossed eight time zones, I was eager to download everything I thought I had learned from Richard Feynman's books, from the UW grad students, from Craig Bohren.

"So, remember when you told me sunlight bounces off water molecules?"

"Uh-huh."

"Well, they don't bounce," I said.

"What do you mean?"

"They are absorbed and reemitted. We just say they bounce because it's easier. Photons always interact with electrons *inside* the atoms."

"Uh-huh."

"And you can't predict exactly where the electrons are at any one time or which photons will be refracted and which reflected or in what direction. Look at our glass coffee table here. We can look *through* the glass and see the rug underneath it. And we can see the reflection of the wine bottle *in* the glass."

My husband looked at the table as if seeing it for the first time. He didn't say anything for a long while. I thought maybe he was falling asleep. It was 3:00 a.m. his body time, after all.

"Interesting. But a glass coffee table is not a cloud droplet," he said.

"But electrons are moving around randomly and all the time in every atom in the glass and in the clouds and in every atom of everything else too. The clouds and the table are similar in that invisible water vapor is like clear glass, and white cloud droplets are like shattered glass. And also like sugar and salt—as individual particles they are clear, but collectively they are white. The same is true with milk, flour, and snow."

"Right, but—hmmm."

There was a long pause. I could tell he thought I was too far down a rabbit hole and that he didn't want to say so. I gave him an easy out.

"So, how was Nigeria?"

"Fine, but understanding the whiteness of clouds at this level is like studying a symphony by examining the individual hairs on a violin bow."

Reluctantly I took his point. I needed to emerge from my rabbit hole (as fascinating as I had found it). Tomorrow, I told him, I'd return to the big, bright beautiful masses of visible cloud droplets. But not before doing a quick internet search: "Do individual hairs on the violin bow matter?"

Guess what! Researchers at the University of Music and Performing Arts in Vienna used scanning-electron microscopes to analyze the fibers of violin bows from six different countries. They published their results in 2007 and concluded that the structural properties of the hairs were different but that those differences had a negligible effect on the sound produced when played. What mattered most to the sound? The rosin violinists rub on their bows.

The Fly

As I was climbing out of my rabbit hole (and side chambers), I sat at my kitchen table typing up my notes on cloud droplets, uncertainty, and the lifestyle of the single electron. It was a sunny afternoon in February and the house was quiet save for a single very loud fly. It was one of those really big flies known as a cluster fly—a black jumbo jet of a fly, the kind that overwinter in the walls of residential houses then come to life on warm winter days. I tried to ignore it.

It bonked its head on the kitchen window and then zipped through the kitchen and bonked its head on the picture window in the living room. It was silent for a while. I refocused on my work and had nearly forgotten about the fly when it returned to the kitchen and strafed my laptop. It bounced off the window, the wall, the other window, the other wall, and the ceiling. I tried swatting at it with a dishtowel but it was fast, its flight path random, and our ceilings vaulted. This fly had a lot of space to elude an encounter.

Rather than continue to chase it, I opened the back door and then sat back down to write. Rather than finding its way outside, the fly buzzed back to the living room and was quiet. I hoped it was preoccupied with mating or nursing its concussions and would leave me alone. But no. Here came the familiar buzz of the incoming beast. It landed on the edge of my laptop screen—right at eye level. Rather than swat at it and risk squashing it on my screen, I held very still and glowered at it.

Its body was covered in stubby little hairs. The tiny facets of its huge compound eyes glinted. It rubbed its front legs together as if it were hatching a nefarious plan. Then it made a forty-five-degree turn, bringing us eye-to-eye. It lingered. It seemed to be staring. I half-expected it to speak—to quote Kafka or Kahlil Gibran or recite a haiku in some squeaky little fly voice. I held very still and waited. It turned and flew back toward the kitchen window—bonk, bonk, bonk—and then out the door and into the sunlight. I turned back to my laptop and to the electrons, amused if not enlightened.

Altostratus

One gloomy winter morning, my husband I were heading downtown. While he drove, I looked out at the clouds—horizon-to-horizon Altostratus. With my polarized sunglasses on, I could see subtle striations of gray indicating the flow of the wind and a bit of brightness revealing the position of the sun.

"See? They're not just solid, unmitigated gray!" I said.

He looked up and around and then burst out laughing.

Altostratus has earned a reputation as the boring cloud, but from my perspective, getting outside and studying a cloud that might be spread over several thousands of square miles is always more interesting than staring up at a truly boring ceiling in my home. What makes Altostratus clouds so interesting is not their gray color but their composition. These clouds are a mix of ice crystals, snowflakes, and even some water droplet clouds embedded in the Altostratus itself. The thickness—typically more than 6,500 feet—prevents these clouds from scattering white sunlight the way more purely white clouds do. Such thick clouds absorb sunlight. When light is absorbed, it is not scattered toward our eyes. What reaches our eyes is a lack of light—that's the gray, a shade of darkness. Altostratus clouds have a distinctive bluish-gray color that makes them easier to distinguish from higher, whiter Cirrostratus clouds from which they often form. "Easier" and not "easy" because Altostratus clouds are classified as mid-level clouds although they can extend into the high-altitude range where the Cirrostratus are found.

Altostratus clouds are generally so uniform in appearance and structure that they have no named species. They do have named varieties, which express subtle differences in their transparency and arrangement, including one that hides the sun completely (Altostratus opacus) and one that allows you to determine—vaguely and as if through ground glass—the sun's position in the sky (Altostratus translucidus) and one that occurs in two layers (Altostratus duplicatus).

Altostratus clouds give me ample opportunity to appreciate the gray, the shades, the nuances, the thin patches I point to while saying facetiously, "Look! It's going to clear up!" More often than not, it does not. Altostratus tend to thicken, descend, and bring on the rain.

Altostratus clouds are capable of precipitating, but the rain or snow that falls from them usually evaporates below the cloud's base before reaching the ground. Oftentimes, the ice crystals and snowflakes from the Altostratus do not evaporate but continue to fall toward the ground as snow or, if the air is warm, as rain. This marks the transition of Altostratus to Nimbostratus. The surest way to tell these two gray, mid-level layer clouds apart is the presences of steady falling rain or snow. In western Washington, where I live, my rule is this: if I'm getting wet, it's Nimbostratus; if not, Altostratus.

On the Bright Side

If you are not fascinated by nuances of gray in Altostratus, you can take advantage of these clouds to improve your photography. Some photographers argue that the low, golden light at sunrise and sunset is the best light for outdoor photography and the *only* light for shooting landscapes. This golden light is indeed beautiful, but it encourages midday napping, disdain for cloudy skies, and missed opportunities for great photos.

Altostratus clouds are actually the photographer's best friend. Because of the mix of droplets and ice in these clouds, they diffuse sunlight and create soft, even lighting ideal for photography. Imagine—no eerily long shadows, no portraits with squinting faces, no predawn alarms, and no racing against the sun. And because Altostratus keep their precipitation to themselves, you don't have to deal with rain or snow on your lenses.

"When the clouds come out and completely cover up the sky, don't weep," writes David Johnston on his Photography Roundtable website, "just fight back by shooting waterfalls! Cloudy skies provide perfect conditions to shoot waterfalls because they completely eliminate distracting shadows, they provide soft light, and you are able to focus on intimate details of landscapes."

Curious, I sent David an email asking for advice on shooting under thick, layered clouds like Altostratus.

"Clouds are great for all detail shots with macro lenses or landscapes with a 70–200 mm lens," he replied. "Basically any shot that doesn't include the sky. I always pray for thick cloud cover for portraits too. If I don't get them, I find solid shade to shoot in."

I have never prayed for thick cloud cover to enhance my photos, but as a writer I have on occasion prayed for Altostratus clouds to eliminate distractions and help me focus on details. Altostratus clouds are the white noise of the sky, the mute button of the atmosphere, the cloud that practically begs you to ignore it. Why, you might ask, would someone writing about clouds want to ignore them? The clouds were my subject—yes—but I couldn't watch them and write about them at the same time. While I was reading or writing about the clouds in my office, I'd invariably notice a sudden change in the light and I'd turn to the window to see what was happening. Something was always happening, something that would lure me outside for a better view. A more disciplined writer would have pulled down the blinds, but I had to look. Often for hours at a time. But not with Altostratus. I knew these thick, grayish layers would stay that thick and gray for most of the day, letting me focus on my writing and not feel I was missing something.

The only time Altostratus proved to be distracting was at sunrise and sunset when the red and orange light from the sun accentuated the corrugated or banded appearance of its undersides. Altostratus are one of the clouds supporting the time-honored adage "Red sky at night, sailors' delight; red sky in morning, sailors take warning."

Dazzling red sunsets can occur when these clouds extend from overhead toward the western horizon where the setting sun—in a band of clear sky—shines through and casts the Altostratus bases in dramatic relief. Since our weather generally moves from west to east around the globe, chances are that that band of clear sky in the west means there is more clear sky behind it moving toward you. The Altostratus will float off eastward.

The reverse is true in the morning, when the Altostratus have moved in from the west overnight and the only clear sky to be found is near the eastern horizon where the rising sun shines through and under the Altostratus. A dazzling Altostratus sunrise makes a great start to a day, but these eastward-moving clouds may soon cover the sky and, as the adage forewarns, develop over the day into lower Nimbostratus—the rain cloud.

Neither Altostratus nor any other clouds get enough credit for their role in spectacular sunrises and sunsets. We ask, "Did you see the sky last night?" or "Wasn't the sunrise beautiful this morning?" What often makes a landscape painting great are its clouds, not necessarily the land; what makes a sunrise and sunset glorious are the clouds, not necessarily the sun. Next time you watch a sunrise or sunset in a cloud-free sky, you'll see what I mean. You might even yawn.

Many types of clouds show off in low light and can display most colors in the visible-light spectrum and in many shades of these colors. Let some of my survey takers explain the science behind one of the most popular cloud colors at sunset—pink.

Cloud Survey Question

 Everyone loves pink clouds, but can you explain why they are pink?

Something with reflection and light and something i don't know.
Reflection of the setting sun?
Haven't really given it much thought. Probably the angle of the sun and horizon, etc.
Sailor's delight?
Because everyone looks good in pink, even men, so God must've had a good sense of color and style.
I always think of a newborn baby's blanket.
They're embarrassed.
It has something to do with the setting of the sun and the reflection of the light.
It has to do with the time of day.
It has to do with dust particles and the angle of the light.
Same reason that we have sunsets, right? (I'm so ashamed.)
No, but I am sure it has to do with the time of day.
A storm is coming.
Probably it's sunset?
Erm—something to do with the angle at which the sun penetrates the atmosphere in the evening and morning?

Um, because the sun is refracting through water droplets?
Because the sky is on fire with my wittiness?
Bending of the light spectrum as the sun goes over the horizon.
To make us feel nice at the end of the day?
Can't explain it, but feel like I have known.

There is a little bit of truth in all of these answers, but only one in sixty-seven respondents offered a reasonable and commendable explanation: "At either sunrise or sunset, the sun is at a very low angle and its rays are being bent and the different wavelengths of light are being spread out. The red ones (longer wavelengths) are not scattered as much as the shorter ones and so they reach our eyes."

A bit of background: Imagine Earth as a leather-covered softball. The leather cover represents the troposphere—the layer of our atmosphere where most of our clouds form. In this layer is an abundance of floating dust, salt, and other particles. You are the sun, and you are holding a straight pin that represents a beam of light. Stab the pin straight down through the leather cover. This is equivalent to sunlight penetrating the atmosphere around noon, traveling straight through the eight miles. Now hold the pin at a low angle (almost horizontally) and try to stab it through the leather. At this low angle (sunrise or sunset), your pin has to penetrate a thicker portion of the leather or more of the lower atmosphere and more of the dust and other particles. The shorter wavelengths (green, blue, indigo, violet) are scattered by these particles. The longer (red, orange, yellow) wavelengths are not scattered and proceed through the atmosphere toward the clouds and our eyes.

Cloud droplets reflect whatever light is shone on them. In this case, the reddish wavelengths dominate the light and so our white clouds turn pink. But not because they are embarrassed.

2

ICE

*A cloud is a visible mass of water droplets or **ice** crystals suspended in the atmosphere above the earth.*

Every definition of "cloud" includes the word "ice," so I had to believe it was true. I knew well the ice that fell out of the clouds as snow, sleet, and hail, but I hadn't given much thought to such stuff staying in the cloud *as* the cloud. That water could freeze and stay frozen in the air between me and the blazing sun seemed inconceivable, especially on hot summer days. Yet there I'd be in shorts and a T-shirt, sweating, and there they'd be—the clouds—in wisps and layers, freezing.

Cirrus and Cirrostratus, two of our highest cloud types, are both composed entirely of ice. Knowing this, I jumped to the conclusion that ice clouds must form in the highest altitude range where the air is the coldest. Not so. The air temperatures at mid- and low altitudes can be cold enough for ice to form in all ten cloud types.

My understanding of ice was, dare I say, not very solid. Lucky for me, my older son had left his college chemistry book at home after his freshman year so I let Dr. Science off the hook this time and started reading.

To become ice, in clouds or at ground level, liquid water has to freeze—meaning the water molecules slow down their fluid jiggling and zinging commotion and lock into crystal structures. The positively charged end of one water molecule (the end where the hydrogen atoms are located) bonds with the negatively charged end of another water molecule (where the "ears" aren't), creating a hydrogen bond. When six water molecules are bonded together this way, they create an open hexagon—a pattern that is repeated regularly as freezing continues. Hexagon by hexagon, frozen water molecules develop into larger and more complex crystal shapes—all based on the hexagon.

At ground level, the freezing point of water is 32°F. One could be forgiven for assuming that this means liquid water freezes and becomes ice at this temperature. It does not, because 32°F is also the *melting* point of water—the temperature at which ice melts and becomes a liquid. How can this be?

In liquid water at 32°F, the formation of each hydrogen bond releases a little bit of heat from the water molecule. This heat is then reabsorbed by the molecule, which causes the hydrogen bond to break. The breaking is what we call melting—the return of the frozen water molecule to its liquid phase. At 32°F, hydrogen bonds form and break at the same rate. Water at this temperature (if well mixed) is said to be in a state of equilibrium.

To get a solid meaningful freeze, the equilibrium has to tip in favor of freezing. This means removing the heat created by the hydrogen bonding by lowering the temperature to below 32°F. How far below? If you are looking to make ice cubes in a few hours, the standard setting on most kitchen freezers—0°F—should do the trick.

If this is the state of affairs in the freezer, it would seem logical that liquid water droplets would behave the same way in the atmosphere—that is, they would begin to freeze at just below 32°F and become solid ice crystals around 0°F. This is not what happens. Liquid water droplets in the atmosphere do not begin freezing until 23°F. The onset of freezing varies and is strongly connected to the size of the water droplets, the temperature of the cloud base, the air temperature, the relative humidity, and other atmospheric conditions. Generally speaking, most of the water droplets in clouds between 32°F and 5°F are still liquid and are known as "supercooled" droplets. Some of these droplets may freeze into ice crystals below 5°F and down to −33°F but not until the temperature dips below this lower temperature do all the supercooled droplets freeze.

Why are supercooled droplets so stubborn?

I had to wonder if water droplets considered "getting iced" a fate worse than death. If I were a liquid water droplet freewheeling in the atmosphere, evaporating and condensing whenever it suited me, I might resist getting locked up in a hexagonal prison too.

Ice Nuclei

Anthropomorphism aside, liquid water droplets in clouds are not stubborn, they just require more than subfreezing temperatures to freeze. They need something to freeze on—something like cloud condensation nuclei but with a surface that mimics the hexagonal structure of ice itself. Such suitable nuclei, called ice nuclei, do exist but are rare—perhaps one per million airborne particles in the atmosphere. So in below freezing temperatures, supercooled droplets have two choices. They can wait it out until just the right ice nuclei comes along, or they can wait a little longer and freeze on their own.

The sources of ice nuclei and their distribution in the atmosphere are still not well known. Scientific research suggests that the maritime clouds forming over the Pacific Ocean may contain ice nuclei formed from phytoplankton, bacteria, and other organisms present in the ocean and transferred into the atmosphere through sea spray. Phytoplankton emit a sulfur compound, dimethyl sulfide, to form aerosols that serve as cloud condensation nuclei and, at subfreezing temperatures, ice nuclei.

One of the most common and effective ice nuclei is a mineral called kaolinite. I had never heard of kaolinite, but my husband, who has a master's degree in geology and remembers everything he learned from sixth grade onward, knew all about it.

"It's known for its whiteness, purity, and fineness," he said. "It's a silicate mined all over the world, mostly for industrial uses. It's what's in porcelain clay, in the glossy coating on paper, rubber, paint, deodorants, makeup—all sorts of things. I'm pretty sure it's the 'kao' in the original Kaopectate."

"So people eat ice nuclei to stop diarrhea?" I asked. "I don't want to think about that."

But I did want to think about porcelain. I had been handling porcelain clay for years in my weekly ceramics class without knowing I might be stealing ice nuclei from the clouds. When I contacted my pottery instructor to share my discovery, she told me that the many types of porcelain we used in class all contained kaolinite and were referred to by clay wholesalers simply as "kaolin." The reason I didn't know this was because we used other names for kaolin in class: "Grolleg" (kaolin from Cornwall, England), "New Zealand" (kaolin from "the land of the long white cloud"), and "JG" (the initials of our instructor, who created this proprietary blend of Grolleg and other clays).

Kaolinite was named in 1637 after the village in China—Gaoling (or Kaoling)—that is considered the type locality for this mineral. Kaolin clay is white, fine, creamy, and smooth and is valued for its fluidity and translucence. There is no scientific evidence that the clouds formed on kaolinite manifest these same qualities, but the two other main types of clay, stoneware and earthenware, are decidedly not cloud-like—they are coarse-grained, hard, tight, and in colors such as brown, yellow, and red. While particles of minerals in these clays could be found in the atmosphere, it seems that kaolinite has the corner on clouds. Like other mineral dust, kaolinite enters the atmosphere as fine particles when the soil or rock where it naturally occurs is disturbed through erosion or mining. Because of its small particle size, the kaolinite dust is found at higher altitudes than other, larger mineral particles, including those present in the stoneware or earthenware clay that ceramicists use.

Many types of mineral particles are light enough to be carried aloft by the wind, but what distinguishes kaolinite as ice nuclei is its crystal structure: "pseudohexagonal." These perfect-enough, microscopic bits of kaolinite are found in relatively high densities where the air is 14°F or lower, temperatures generally found above 10,000 feet. Here the supercooled water droplets are ready to freeze on these ice nuclei and build their tiny hexagonal empires.

Without ice nuclei, supercooled droplets can freeze spontaneously. "Spontaneous" in this context does not mean "in a fun-loving, impulsive way" but instead "without external influence," which in this scientific context would be a speck of phytoplankton, kaolinite, or other particle. What happens spontaneously is that enough water molecules *within* the water droplet freeze to form a tiny mass known as an ice embryo, which serves as an ice nucleus. These ice embryos can form just below the freezing temperature, but they break apart easily when weakened by the heat released as the liquid water freezes. Not until the air is colder than −33°F is that heat removed from the droplet with adequate efficiency to allow spontaneous freezing.

Ice crystals can also form through "riming and splintering," which is not a technique used by jazz singers but a process of freezing. Rime is a thin coating of ice (similar to frost at ground level) that forms when supercooled water droplets collide with ice crystals and freeze onto them. This produces a soft hail-like pellet known as graupel. As the graupel falls and captures cloud droplets, some of the droplets, while freezing, emit splinters of ice, which in turn freeze to other cloud droplets, setting off a chain reaction of splintering and freezing that creates ice-crystal clouds.

No one should underestimate the creativity of water.

Cirrostratus

I have not told you the whole truth about my morning, so many years ago now, spent in the dim hall with Art Rangno's cloud poster. I wasn't captivated by all the clouds equally that morning but by just one cloud in particular. It was an unphotogenic smear of a cloud tucked behind a dull patch of alpine scenery. The foreground of the photo was dominated by a two-lane highway splotched with shadows.

What a bad photograph, I thought. It looked like the work of an amateur—a Sunday driver who had pulled off the road to photograph a chipmunk, missed the chipmunk, but captured the empty road and unwittingly some clouds. None of the other photographs in the poster were so poorly composed, no foreground so ugly. I looked to the caption for an explanation. "CIRROSTRATUS (fibratus): It had been a good vacation day. Rounding the corner, however, you become upset. You see the solid layer of high, icy clouds on the western horizon. You know that the weather will deteriorate. The perfect sunlight will be dimmed within an hour, and it may rain within 24."

How very odd, I thought.

A "good vacation day" and "perfect sunlight" didn't belong in this poster. Neither did anyone who was "upset." "You become upset." You who? Why was the unscientific second-person voice used here? Who wrote this strange caption and why? Was this a private joke between the caption writer and a certain someone who had once overreacted to an ice cloud? Suddenly I wanted to be that someone. I didn't want to overreact but simply to know the clouds well enough to be able to respond to them emotionally or intellectually when they appeared in my life.

I reread the quirky caption and stared at the lackluster Cirrostratus cloud in the photograph. I recalled lines from Rod Serling's opening narration of the TV show *The Twilight Zone*: "You're moving into a land of both shadow and substance, of things and ideas. . . .You unlock this door with the key of imagination."

During my first conversation with Art Rangno I asked him why he wrote the caption for the Cirrostratus cloud in such an "unusual style."

His answer came instantly.

"To see if anyone was paying attention!"

He sounded exasperated, a bit outraged. I asked for an explanation.

Art told me of his disappointment when he discovered that his posters were being used mainly as décor. They hung in offices, classrooms, and on doors where they were briefly admired and then ignored. He suspected no one was reading his text. If this were true, Art guessed, they weren't learning anything about the clouds. And this really bothered him.

To test his theory, Art began slipping offbeat photos and captions into his posters. One morning, while working on the 2000 edition of his poster (the one I had seen), he read about a rash of shootings on the Los Angeles freeways caused by "road rage." He began thinking about people's emotions being so dangerously close to the surface that they easily overreacted. Suddenly an idea erupted in his mind. What would happen, he wondered, if a motorist got upset by a certain kind of cloud instead of by another driver? That's how the road and the Cirrostratus cloud—a harbinger of rain—ended up on his poster. It had been several years since this edition of his poster was published and no one had commented on the photo or the caption.

"You are the only person who's ever asked about it," he told me.

I didn't know what to say to this.

Looking back, being the only person to ever inquire about the idea behind a poster caption wasn't anything to get excited about, but I felt a personal connection to that cloud.

No Cirrostratus has ever been as riveting to me as the one in the *Guide to the Sky*. Cirrostratus, like its cousin Altostratus, is not generally a riveting type of cloud. It is a transparent, whitish, ice-crystal cloud occurring between 16,500 and 45,000 feet. Its appearance is often described as a thin milky veil, although it can be so thin that it is more of a sensation, a perception, than an appearance. Sitting outside on a blue-sky day sometimes, you can detect the merest softening of sunlight or notice the sky has turned a slightly paler shade of blue. The atmosphere seems to have powered down a few kilowatts. Put on your polarizing sunglasses and you'll see a thin gossamer film across the sky. Cirrostratus clouds have arrived.

Not all Cirrostratus clouds are subtle, but most are easy to overlook, even easier to ignore. When they try to vary their appearance, they manage only to compound their relatively dull qualities. Cirrostratus nebulosus shows no variation whatsoever. Cirrostratus duplicatus doubles the dullness into two separate layers. The wavelike undulations of Cirrostratus undulatus are about as exciting as wrinkles in a tablecloth. Even Cirrostratus fibratus makes me want to yawn. But a road-rage cloud? Now *that's* a compelling cloud.

Collecting Clouds

In my first year of cloud watching around Olympia and western Washington, I took thousands of digital photographs of clouds, which I downloaded onto my computer. I did not take the time to change each photo's default name, such as "IMG_5388," or the names of the default folders, such as "124__03."

To organize this mess and to test my cloud identification skills, I eventually created ten new folders—Stratus, Cumulus, Nimbostratus, and the rest. Once I opened the first folder of photos to drag and drop, I realized the horrible truth: paying close attention to the clouds does not guarantee you can identify them.

My first cloud stumped me—Altocumulus or a Cirrocumulus? The second— Cirrus maybe? And the third—no clue. Before long, I had cloud guides on each knee and cloud charts spread out on the floor next to me. There was no way to confirm the accuracy of any of my classifications. There were no green check marks accompanied by happy bell sounds or red Xs with jolting buzzes when I dropped my photos into one of the ten folders. It was all guesswork.

Taking a less ambitious approach, I created three new folders—Layered, Heaped, Wispy—but this gross-level sorting also proved too challenging. Many of my photos seemed to include more than one type of cloud. I created a fourth folder—Mixed. And then a fifth—BWJ (Big White Jobs). A sixth— UFO (for Unidentified Floating Objects)—is where most of my first set of clouds landed, which made my whole sorting exercise pointless.

To bring some sense of order to the chaos, I created twelve folders, one for each month of the year. Perhaps, I thought, a chronological ordering scheme would reveal hidden patterns or seasonality in my local clouds. I dragged and dropped for a few hours. When my husband got home from work, I told him about my cloud-sorting project.

He paused thoughtfully.

"What's the difference between a February and March cloud?"

"I don't know yet. That's why I'm sorting them this way. To see if there is a pattern."

"Hmmm," he said.

He was right.

Monthly was arbitrary. Sorting them by season would make more sense, but I'd need more than a few years' worth of photos to see any pattern.

The next morning, I dragged all my monthly folders into another folder—CLOUDS.

Not long after this, my computer crashed. The diagnosis from the repairman was "too many photographs." My mother lode of cloud photos had left the computer operating system with no room to update itself, stay on top of viruses, and run smoothly.

My husband suggested I start deleting photos.

I told him I could not.

Where would I begin? I could never delete my Altocumulus with the five names. Or the Mother's Day photo of me and my two sons against a sky full of gorgeous mare's tail Cirrus clouds. Or the Cumulonimbus that looked like a giant flying over the Black Hills west of Olympia. Or any of the pink ones. Or the one of me pretending to eat fog on Mount Rainier. Certainly not any of the BWJs, Mixed, or March clouds. What if I had captured a rare cloud no meteorologist had ever seen?

When I used the word "agony" to describe this culling process, my husband chuckled and suggested I store all my photos in "the cloud."

I gave him a look.

"Clouds evaporate," I said.

A few days later, he brought home a backup hard drive the size of a paperback. Now all my clouds are housed together in this small gray box under my desk, as secure and orderly as any clouds will ever be.

I never followed through on making my own local cloud poster. It was just too hard to choose the few dozen best photos from my collection. Besides, I had Art Rangno's posters as permanent installations in my home. The poster on my fridge catches the attention of friends, neighbors, plumbers, electricians, house sitters, and others who walk into my kitchen. "Cool poster!" they usually say after a cursory glance. I always feel some of Art Rangno's disappointment when they don't linger to read or remark on any particular cloud.

The poster in my office serves a different purpose. It hangs next to the window, and when I am working at my desk, I look out the window often to see what is happening in the sky. Clouds are almost always happening. Whether or not I can identify the clouds by name, I rise from my chair to find a match for the clouds outside. And in so doing, I end up lingering, looking at the other clouds on the poster like they were old friends. Thinking back to my first encounter with *A Guide to the Sky*, when I had been waiting so impatiently, I always feel a renewed sense of gratitude for the clouds—for the distraction they provided me that morning and for their abiding presence in my life ever since.

CRYSTALS

A cloud is a visible mass of water droplets or ice **crystals** *suspended in the atmosphere above the earth.*

Hexagonal ice crystals do not form in an orderly fashion, one side of the hexagon at a time, the way you might draw it on paper. Water in the atmosphere freezes in a more chaotic way, with many hexagons forming simultaneously, often in several different planes and with constant interruptions as the hydrogen bonds break in the process of freezing.

Hexagon by hexagon, larger and more elaborate crystals form. The crystal shapes we can't see—the microscopic building blocks of snowflakes—have been classified into ten types: plates, stellars, columns, needles, spatial dendrites, capped columns, irregular crystals, graupel, sleet, and hail. Each crystal forms under very specific and narrow temperature ranges, often of just several degrees.

The difference in appearance of ice crystals and water droplets in a cloud is easiest to observe in Cumulonimbus because you can see the entire cloud in one view. The sharply defined edges of these clouds often indicate the presence of droplets. When these edges soften and appear fibrous or wispy, that's the look of ice. The appearance of this ice, by the way, is what distinguishes Cumulonimbus from the cauliflower-topped Cumulus congestus.

The more subtle Cirrocumulus clouds first form as supercooled droplet clouds, which almost instantly evaporate unless the liquid droplets freeze, in

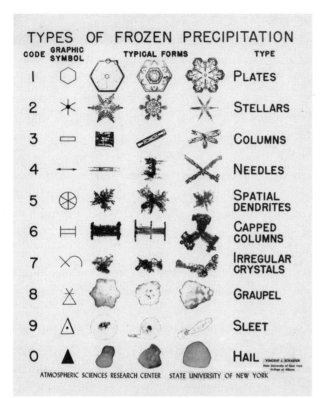

The ice crystals in clouds assume many forms; this chart, published in 1951, shows ten basic types. (Chart by Vincent Schaefer)

which case the ice crystals quickly grow too large or heavy to remain in the cloud. Overcome by gravity, they fall out of the cloud and into lower, warmer air where they become true Cirrus clouds. These ice crystals in these Cirrus, in turn, may evaporate. Or they may fall into slower winds and trail out behind their parent cloud, which moves apace above them. Some crystals will make it all the way to the ground as precipitation. Snowflakes, for instance, are aggregations of many different crystal types and fall to the ground softly, often like downy feathers. Hail, on the other hand, often begins its life as a raindrop that freezes and builds as supercooled water droplets and ice crystals freeze onto its surface. As hailstones rise and fall on the upward and downward air currents in Cumulonimbus clouds, they can grow from the size of a BB to that of a softball and hit the ground with a damaging force.

Sunlight in Ice

One afternoon, when I remembered to look up during my twenty-step walk from my front door to my car, I saw something I used to describe as a "rainbow-like thing" in a cloud. The sky was completely blue except for some ethereal wisps of Cirrus, including one directly overhead that looked like the X-ray of a human rib cage, complete with sternum. As if this wasn't strange enough, three of six ribs—and only the left ribs—of this otherwise white cloud were different colors. One rib was a pinkish-orange, the second a greenish-blue, and the third a violet-blue. It was as if each rib had been individually painted. Looking around, I noticed that the few other streaks of Cirrus were completely white. There was no evidence that the colors I was seeing were part of a larger phenomenon such as a glory or a rainbow. I stood in my driveway and watched until the colors and the cloud faded away.

I had no idea what I had seen, even though I had seen these bits of prismatic light in the sky throughout my life. They often appeared as a ring around the sun, sometimes as an arc or disc nearby it. They were always beautiful, surprising, even magical. I half-understood the science behind rainbows but not how ice crystals created their own special optical phenomena.

These phenomena have various names—including sun dog, tangent arc, upper tangent arc, circumzenithal arc, sun pillar, 22° halo, and 46° halo. Each phenomenon is associated with a particular type of ice crystal and, in some cases, a particular size and orientation of the crystal. Your ability to see them depends on the angle of the sun and your position in relation to the sun.

My favorite displays are sun dogs, which are also called mock suns and parhelia (meaning "with the sun"). I prefer the term "sun dogs" because I love the image of these discs of light—which usually appear in pairs, one on either side of the sun—as two faithful dogs next to their master. Sun dogs appear in icy clouds (especially Cirrostratus, Altostratus, and even jet contrails) when the hexagonal plate crystals larger than 30 micrometers across fall with their large, flat surface parallel to the ground, and when the sun is low in the sky (40 degrees or less above the horizon). Sunlight enters one of the six vertical sides of the hexagon and is refracted, separated into the spectrum of visible colors, and then refracted back out through another side of the crystal—and into the cloud to the left or right of the sun.

Sun dogs flee when the hexagonal plates start to wobble gently from side to side like a falling leaf. If the wobbling occurs around sunrise or sunset, the sunlight may reflect off the tilted surfaces (both top and bottom) of the hexagonal plate without passing through its interior. In this case, you may see a sun pillar—a column-shaped beam of orange sunlight above and below the sun. Sun pillars can be seen in Cirrostratus and Cirrus and also in lower Altocumulus when ice crystals fall from its base.

Sun dogs, sun pillars, and other such phenomena may last for a few hours or just a few moments. The sun angle shifts. Winds carry the clouds out of alignment between you and the sun. The clouds thicken and thin. Ice crystals wobble, realign, aggregate, melt, and evaporate. Look while it lasts.

Warning: Truth be told, no one should be looking directly at these phenomena in the first place. Because these alluring spectacles appear very close to the sun, even a glimpse of the sun presents a serious risk of eye damage. Even if the cloud layer partly masks the sun, it will not protect your eyes. I didn't know all of this until quite recently while reading about these optical phenomena. I was a bit surprised to discover my pursuit of the clouds came with risks to my personal well-being. Of course, there is a risk of being struck by lightning while standing outside during a thunderstorm, but being struck by sunlight while looking at ice crystals wasn't something I had ever worried about.

I decided to err on the side of caution and find out how to mitigate my risks. Some books advise looking at the reflection of the phenomenon in a piece of glass, painted black. When I tried this using picture-frame glass and acrylic paint, my sun dogs were lost in a dark, streaky mess that was decidedly not phenomenal. The dark screen of my cell phone provides a much clearer reflection of the clouds, but the sun dogs were so bright as to be blinding. Another book suggested getting your eye doctor's recommendation for the best dark glasses for you and your cloud-watching lifestyle. If you find yourself caught without such glasses, you can hold up your hand or duck behind a tree to block the sun (but not the nearby phenomenon itself).

I have found it impossible to avoid looking at the sun accidentally when looking at the optical phenomena. Yes, the sun does follow a regular path across the sky and we *should* know its general location during the day, but we are only human. We lose track of time, we get turned around, we forget where we are. A phenomenal display of ice crystals catches our eye and—oops—we are looking right into the sun. Do be careful.

Cloud Survey Question

 What type of cloud is this?

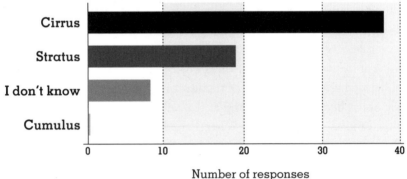

Number of responses

Cirrus

Cirrus clouds form between 16,500 and 45,000 feet and are generally composed of very small ice crystals. Unlike Cirrostratus clouds, which appear in smoother layers, Cirrus appear sparsely as delicate white filaments or in patches or bands. Cirrus are classified as precipitating clouds because of the fallout of ice crystals from them. This ice does not reach the ground except at very high elevations, where it can be felt as the lightest of precipitation, known as "diamond dust."

Even if you've never laid eyes on a horse you can probably recognize mare's tails. You could argue that these long, wispy Cirrus clouds resemble the tails of stallions, colts, geldings, ponies, donkeys, and mules too, but "mare's tails" seems more fitting and fluid, with its airy vowel sounds and Z-like S sounds—much more fitting than its scientific and rarely uttered full name, "Cirrus uncinus." Pronounced *un*-sin-us, it does not mean tail-like, horse-like, or hairlike, but hooked. There seems to be nothing hook-like about this cloud, and I felt its Latin name should have been Cirrus equinus. Then I spoke with my meteorologist.

He pointed out that Cirrus uncinus begins as a subtle little tuft of cloud—a clump of ice crystals—at Cirrus heights, where the winds can range between 100 and 150 mph. As the larger crystals within the tuft become too large or heavy to remain in the cloud, they fall out of the tuft and into the slower winds beneath it. When the first crystals begin falling, the trail is short and *does* appear hooked, like a comma. One of the challenges of catching a young Cirrus uncinus is that they are not always eye-catching in their early stage of development. By the time we do notice them, as long mare's tails stretching out across the sky, the hook shape and the original tuft are often long gone.

Similar in appearance to Cirrus uncinus are the trails of ice known as virga, or fall streaks, which appear beneath most of the ten cloud types (all but Cirrus, Cirrostratus, and Stratus). Virga is not a species or variety of cloud. Nor is it an optical phenomenon. It is a supplementary feature of a cloud. When a cloud shows virga, it is considered a precipitating cloud, although the ice or droplets never reach the ground. Virga, in other words, is a kind of precipitation.

I was curious if the name "virga" had been chosen because this form of precipitation is not sullied by contact with Earth. My printed *Oxford English Dictionary* does not even include the word. The online edition does but skimps on the etymology, stating merely that "virga" is Latin for "rod." This word struck me as too solid and straight for the ethereal, often curving ice crystal trails. When I complained to my meteorologist, he suggested that the curves were likely a matter of perspective because crystals do fall out initially at an almost vertical angle.

All of this makes me wonder: when is what falls out of a cloud no longer part of the cloud? Once all of the ice crystals have fallen behind the original tuft of a Cirrus uncinus, is that cloud of trailing ice crystals still a Cirrus uncinus? Or is it another species with virga? When does this cloud lose its identity as a cloud and exist simply as a "feature," a legacy of its decay? The lines in the sky are difficult to draw.

Cloud Survey Question

 Can you identify these types of clouds? Do you know how they are formed? (The round thing is a moon, not a cloud.)

Cirrus.

Altocumulus.

Stratus.

Looks like they were PhotoShopped.

Wind and jet stream.

Vapor rising from the surface?

Airplanes.

Smog?

Plane exhaust.

Nope, but I like them.

I could make up some smart-ass response (tempting), but I will leave this one a simple "I don't have a clue."

Stratus? No. But the moon was formed when an asteroid slammed into the earth and slammed a chunk loose. At least that's one theory I've heard.

I don't know, but they are pretty.

Nope, but the tree looks like a Douglas-fir.

Don't know the cloud, but the tree is a Western Hemlock.

Stratus? Glad I recognized the moon and Doug-fir.

*Stratus clouds? Occurs when warm moist air ripples up and down,
     causing condensation b/c of variations in temperature? Now that I
     say that, it makes no sense to me.*
   Oh, I don't know.
   Wait, these are clouds?

Yes, these are long, narrow clouds. The tree is a Western hemlock. Yes, these clouds are pretty. No, I did not Photoshop the clouds. And yes, as the responses indicate, these clouds can be tricky to identify.

They are contrails (condensation trails), and they are produced from the exhaust of a jet engine. Contrails and exhaust are not synonymous, however. Contrails are white clouds formed from the water vapor and particles in the exhaust. They occur as single and double trails that appear in crisscrossing and parallel lines in the sky. Airplane exhaust itself is generally transparent or blackish-gray and does not always form contrails.

Jet engine exhaust spews water vapor, unburned fuel, and particles of soot into the atmosphere. On the runway, this might appear as black "smoke" or iridescent clouds of fumes. Higher in the atmosphere—usually above 30,000 feet, where air temperatures are −22°F or lower—the water vapor in the exhaust condenses, using the soot particles and other aerosols in the exhaust as condensation nuclei. Under certain atmospheric conditions, cloud droplets or ice crystals (or both) will form two unnaturally straight, thin white clouds (one from each jet engine) behind the plane. Sometimes these contrails evaporate soon after they form, but sometimes they linger in the sky. In fact, the World Meteorological Organization classifies contrails that have persisted for at least ten minutes as Cirrus homogenitus, a newly introduced Latin term indicating that the cloud is not a "natural" Cirrus cloud but one that forms as a consequence of human activity.

It's easy to tell a Cirrus cloud from a contrail when the plane producing the cloud is flying just ahead of it. Identification gets trickier when the plane is out of sight and the contrails change shape and start to resemble other clouds.

On several occasions I have seen contrails twisted by the wind into a shape similar to the double-helix pattern of strands of human DNA. I have seen the same contrail strands broken into segments that looked like pairs of chromosomes. Once a wide, wind-spread contrail followed me down I-5 from Seattle to Olympia—a distance of sixty miles. It was hard to keep my eyes on the road so I exited and pulled into a gas station to get a few photographs. I sent them to my meteorologist—thinking at the time that I had witnessed a rare or never-before-seen cloud. Nope. Just a surreal contrail and a playful atmosphere.

At the Olympia's Farmers Market one Saturday, I got distracted from my shopping by an eye-catching poster of clouds.

"Will you sign our petition to stop the government from spraying us with chemicals," asked one of the three people standing near the poster.

I looked up into the blue sky in surprise.

"Well, they're not spraying today," one woman said quickly, "but most other days the skies are covered in chemtrails and we need to stop them."

These sky watchers don't use the term "contrails," but "chemtrails" because they believe they contain chemical toxins and pollutants that the US government is intentionally spraying on its citizenry. I suggested ever so gently that jet-fuel exhaust was being emitted from planes all the time during flight and that the contrails appeared only under certain atmospheric conditions and at certain altitudes. She looked like a deer in the headlights.

"Well, I don't know about that, but there's a scientist in California who knows all about this. There's research. You can look her up. Her name is Catherine—or, wait, I think it's Christine."

She turned to the other women.

"What's her name?"

"Rosalind," one said as she handed me a flyer. "HOW DO YOU LIKE YOUR SKIES . . . NATURAL OR MAN-MADE?" The use of all uppercase letters and the outsized question mark in a puffy blue font undermined this group's credibility. Beneath the big loud question were photographs of crisscrossing contrails and dead trees supposedly killed by them.

"The government is spraying us with toxic chemicals," the first woman continued while I read. "They are polluting our land and water, and we need to stop them. Will you sign our petition?"

"I'd like to look into the issue a little more," I said as I moved on to pick up some Washington State apples—organic, unsprayed.

The website of this particular group featured articles and video clips by the aforementioned "scientist" (a retired agricultural crop loss adjustor), links to thirty-five thousand articles and reports on weather modification (and on toxic toys, honey bees, and something called fluoroquinolones), and a PowerPoint presentation that included a list of all the alleged side effects of chemtrails: "Fatigue, Allergies, Memory Loss, Respiratory Problems, Raspy Voice, Sore Throats, Headaches, Dizziness, Skin Rashes, Rickets, Nose Bleeds, Eye Irritations, Agricultural Crop Losses, Backyard Garden Declines, Tree Decline, and Tree Deaths!" Didn't traveling hucksters sell snake oil to cure many of these same problems in the nineteenth century?

The website featured an image of a "black chemtrail," a sight I have seen on many occasions and know to be nothing more than a harmless shadow of a contrail cast onto a layer of cloud.

The contrails were just the tip of the iceberg. The main concern of these citizens is geoengineering—the deliberate, large-scale, technological modification of the environment to combat the effects of climate change. Geoengineering is the real name for a real and relatively new field of science but one with international support and funding, research programs, and university courses at undergraduate and graduate levels. For several years, geoengineering has been the focus of various working groups of the Intergovernmental Panel on Climate Change. Geoengineering includes, among other things, modifying the weather, the clouds, and the quantity and quality of aerosols in the atmosphere. Jet contrails, these conspiracy theorists suggest, are part of the US government's geoengineering efforts—ones that are unregulated, unmonitored, potentially dangerous, and full of unintended negative consequences.

What disturbs me about these theorists is not their lack of scientific evidence to support their claims of a "spraying" program but instead their lack of imagination for what water and ice are capable of in the atmosphere. Condensed water vapor appears in myriad forms in our skies, and one form is contrails. The fact that jet airplanes are in front of them makes the planes a smoking gun, and this makes it easy to blame the federal government and commercial airlines in general for polluting our air, water, and soil—which, of course, they are. But are they "spraying us" intentionally with potentially harmful chemicals? No and yes.

No, because the pollution created by airplane exhaust is a matter of thoughtlessness, carelessness, or willful disregard for the serious and negative environmental impacts of burning fossil fuels. Pollutant-bearing contrails are a visible side effect of jet flight, a by-product of combustion. Whether you can see an airplane's contrails or not, that plane is pumping pollutants (and water vapor) into the sky on every single flight. As a passenger on several of these flights a year, I am contributing to this problem.

Yes, because since World War II, the US government has been experimenting with adding chemicals into the clouds to increase rainfall during drought, reduce the size of hailstones damaging to agricultural crops, and eliminate fog from airports and highways. The chemicals—dry ice, silver iodide, and salt— are sprayed into clouds or released from the ground to create ice crystals in clouds in the hopes that more ice crystals would lead to more snow and rain on the ground. For decades, these cloud-seeding technologies have been used strategically by the US military to generate cloud cover, fog, and flooding rains to give troops a strategic advantage—and to put enemies at a disadvantage.

Other cloud-seeding experiments are designed to combat drought in agricultural areas, but none of the expensive cloud-seeding experiments have been proven successful. During his career as a research meteorologist, Art Rangno published in scientific journals many articles and critiques of cloud-seeding experiments. In most experiments, he writes, it is not clear "whether more precipitation is reaching the ground than would occur naturally." The "problem is [that] you can't really tell what you did when natural precipitation is occurring without . . . long (read, expensive) randomized experiments."

Thin, nonprecipitating clouds that are seeded absolutely can produce precipitation, Art tells me, but this very slight precipitation hardly seems worth the huge cost of seeding.

Whether or not the government is "spraying" us intentionally, whether or not what is being sprayed is causing rain, no one can doubt the well-established science that proves that airplane exhaust—and pretty much every form of combusted fossil fuel—is polluting our air, soil, and water and everything living in it and is contributing to human health problems. We have sacrificed much in our pursuit of flight and our drive to control the skies. Let's hope our scientists fully understand the negative side effects, the unintended consequences, and the real costs of any solution they propose to clean up the mess we have made of our atmosphere and climate.

Strange Skies

A neighbor sent me a text message one afternoon: "Freaky cloud outside. Quick." I walked out my front door, and there it was, right in front of me—a

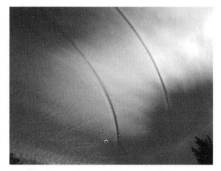

Trails of evaporating ice crystals turn this layer of Cirrocumulus cloud into a mystery.

wide patch of cloud with two arcing, parallel gashes through the middle of it. Through the gashes I could see blue sky.

The cloud was a patch of normal-looking Cirrocumulus, but the gashes were very strange. I had never seen such a sight, nor could I imagine how the gashes had gotten there. (Orion with a machete? Tracks from the *Polar Express* train? Wind shear?) I sent my meteorologist the photos I took and a note: "What's going on here?"

He identified them as "distrails," short for "dissipation trails."

Like contrails, distrails are caused by jet planes, but where contrails are streaks of white cloud in blue sky, distrails are streaks of blue sky in a white cloud. The dissipation of the cloud is caused by evaporation. From their location and the direction of the path of the gashes, I guessed that the plane or planes that made them had taken off—one right after the next—from Portland, one hundred miles to the south, and had encountered the cloud over Olympia as they climbed toward their cruising altitude. My meteorologist had another theory.

A double distrail like mine, he said, could only have been caused by two planes—probably military jets—flying in close proximity above the cloud, not through it. There were a few ways these distrails could have formed, he suggested. The heat from the planes' exhaust could have caused the evaporation. Or (because clouds never do things just one way), the air flowing off the wing tips of the planes (and merging behind them) could have circulated the drier air above down into the cloud.

Or if the water in these clouds had been supercooled, that is, at temperatures well below freezing already, the cooler air moving over the wings of the plane could have further cooled these droplets, and two trails of ice crystals would have formed bright-white contrails—brighter than the cloud. That brightness would have faded as the ice crystals spread out and then fell below the original cloud—leaving a sky-blue path in their wake.

Distrails are rare, my meteorologist told me. Seeing two parallel distrails is even rarer. In a decade of watching the skies, I have never again seen such a sight.

SUSPENDED

*A cloud is a visible mass of water droplets or ice crystals **suspended** in the atmosphere above the earth.*

I would have preferred to float rather than suspend my clouds, but "suspended" appeared more often in my collection of "cloud" definitions, so I accepted it reluctantly.

"Suspended" implies there is something suspending the cloud. When masses of water droplets or ice crystals weighing as much as a sofa, a car, forty elephants, or a jumbo jet are suspended over your head, it's good to know how their suspension system works. Just what that system *was* was not part of any of the definitions I had read.

"Suspend" is from two Latin words—*sus*, meaning "up," and *pendere*, meaning "to cause something to hang." "Suspend" is a verb, but "suspended" in the context of clouds is an adjective—one that describes something (the mass, the cloud) that is "held up without attachment, or held aloft."

What suspends the water droplets and ice crystals in the clouds is buoyancy. I knew that boats and buoys and corks were buoyant, but this did not help me with the clouds. Boats, buoys, and corks float in water. Clouds do not. I read in my old *Webster's New Collegiate Dictionary* that buoyancy is the "tendency of a body to float or rise when submerged in a fluid." In the same way I usually thought of water as a liquid, I also thought of fluid as liquids, as in "drink plenty of fluids." In fact, air is a fluid—something that yields easily to pressure and is capable of flowing without separating. A fluid did not have to be wet. Now I could understand that a cloud was buoyant because it floated in a fluid. Which was weird and fun to think about in a circular logic kind of way, until I realized I wasn't moving forward with my definition.

What causes a cloud's buoyancy?

Buoyancy can be explained partly by the fact that a cloud is less dense than the air below it. The densities of clouds vary, but an average Cumulus cloud contains 0.5 grams of water per cubic meter. The density of air varies, but at standard atmospheric conditions—at sea level and at 59°F—dry air weighs a whopping 1,275 grams per cubic meter—that's 2,250 times the weight of the water in a cloud of these same dimensions.

So there is the fact of density and the tendency of buoyancy. Was the air or the cloud actually *doing* anything in their relationship?

The closest I could get to an action verb was the heavy "lifting" done by the water vapor molecules when they condense into liquid droplets and release a tiny bit of energy known as the "latent" (hidden) heat of condensation. This heat keeps the molecules, the droplets, and the entire cloud suspended.

Not a Flotation Device

I had lunch one day with a family friend—an intelligent woman in her early seventies. She filled me in on her travels, her children, and grandchildren. And she asked about my family and my writing about clouds.

She listened thoughtfully and ate her sandwich while I talked. Then she put her sandwich down and looked at me straight in the eye as if she was about to make a confession.

"Is there any kind of a cloud," she began, "that, for any reason or—in any circumstance, could be capable of supporting—or even possibly holding up a person? I mean—could a person ever sit or lie down in a cloud in such a way that they would not fall through?"

I was about to laugh, but she was not joking. I shook my head no—slowly and sympathetically to ease her disappointment. I sensed that my answer might tarnish her vision of heaven, with its cloud-dwelling angels, cherubim, and seraphim.

My friend's question was a good one—one that we have all likely thought about but not dared to ask. My "no" wasn't a matter of religious beliefs. When it comes to imagining the unimaginable—what happens to us after death—it's anyone's guess. As to the practicality of floating in the clouds for eternity, I believe science will override the ideas of art and religion.

"Clouds do look dense," I told my friend, "but they are mostly tiny droplets of water, water vapor, air, and empty space. A body would fall right through."

She seemed a bit crestfallen.

"You might," I added, "be able to get swept up in the updraft of a storm cloud for a short while, but a cloud could never hold you up the way a sofa would."

"I didn't think so," she said matter-of-factly as she picked up her sandwich and resumed eating.

And then I told her the story of a cloud that did hold someone aloft for what must have felt like an eternity.

In the Cloud

There is no dearth of spine-tingling tales from airplane pilots, meteorologists, sailors, hang gliders, or hot-air balloonists chronicling their extraordinary encounters with clouds. The intent of this book is to offer stories of everyday clouds—clouds I have observed personally and through ordinary means.

However, there is one story—true, unique, and nearly unbelievable—that I would be remiss for not including. It is the story of a jet-fighter pilot and the Cumulonimbus that grabbed him and would not let go. The pilot, William Rankin, survived the 1959 encounter and published a book about it the following year. *The Man Who Rode the Thunder* is long out of print and were it not for a recent retelling in *The Cloudspotter's Guide*, this story might have been lost to modern readers. My very condensed version here, based on Rankin's book, focuses on his vivid descriptions of the cloud both during and after his ordeal. But first I must get his plane aloft.

On July 26, 1959, Lt. Col. William H. Rankin, a 39-year-old US Marine Corps pilot, prepared to fly an F8U Crusader jet fighter from South Weymouth, Massachusetts, to Beaufort, North Carolina. It was a routine flight—a distance of 800 miles—and would take just seventy minutes. Rankin wore a summer-weight flight suit (not his pressurized one), gloves, helmet, oxygen mask connected to the plane's supply, and parachute pack with enough oxygen to last five or ten minutes.

Rankin took off around 5:30 p.m. and headed south. As he approached Norfolk, Virginia, he began a steady, easy climb over Cumulonimbus clouds ahead. The clouds, which Rankin refers to only as "thunderheads" or simply "clouds" throughout his memoir, were taller than he expected. At 45,000 feet he passed through their icy, wispy tops, and then noticed his plane slowing.

He nosed down a thousand feet to pick up speed for a climb back up over the cloud top. When he started climbing again, he heard a strange thump and rumbling sounds coming from his plane. A warning light flashed "FIRE." His radio crackled and died. Then the engine quit. Rankin attempted to engage the auxiliary engine, but the handle came off in his hand, almost like a scene in a cartoon. Rankin had two choices: he could go down with the plane in a fatal spin at supersonic speed or eject himself.

At exactly 6:00 p.m., less than twenty seconds after first sensing his plane troubles, Rankin pulled the ejection seat handles. An explosive charge sent him into the air at several hundred miles an hour. The air was –70°F. The temperature and the explosive decompression pressure turned Rankin's body into a "freezing, expanding mass of pain." Exposed parts of his body stung with cold and then went numb.

Everything began to spin like a kaleidoscope. The sun went by in blurred, reddish-orange streaks. He was tumbling and cartwheeling through space in a 120-mph free fall. Rankin soon entered the "undulating, milky-white fields" of ice at the glaciated top of the Cumulonimbus. As he descended, Rankin felt the air getting heavier and more comfortable to breathe. He knew his parachute barometer was set to open at 10,000 feet, which it did, with a sudden and violent lurch. Rankin's descent slowed. Looking up from within the cloud, he could see only the taut risers leading from his body harness to the canopy of the parachute. The parachute itself was hidden in the cloud.

Rankin took off his oxygen mask and started to relax. He rose and fell gently in the slightly turbulent air in the cloud. He was in fierce pain but overjoyed to be alive and coherent. He calculated that, falling at the rate of 1,000 feet per minute, he'd reach the ground in about ten minutes and his ordeal would be over. Then the fury and the physics of the Cumulonimbus caught up with him.

Violent updrafts and downdrafts yanked him up and down repeatedly as if he were on a series of high-speed elevator rides. He moved ever deeper in "an angry ocean of boiling clouds, blacks and grays and whites, spilling over each other, into each other, digesting each other." Rankin described himself as "a veritable molecule trapped in the thermal pattern of [a] heat engine." He was buffeted in all directions, rattled violently, and pushed around by g-forces as if he were a "bag of flesh and bones crashing into a concrete floor, an empty human shell soaring, a lifeless form strangely suspended in air. . . . I felt as if I were not only fighting for my life, but my sanity as well."

Rankin and his parachute spun together and over each other as if in a giant tandem somersault. His parachute collapsed and billowed. At one point, a violent blast of air sent him up inside the canopy, which then collapsed over him before it billowed again.

As a trained pilot, Rankin knew how thermals and convection cycles worked in the atmosphere. He knew that the rising air he was trapped in would "spill over" the top of the cloud and sink downward on the outside of the cloud. He hoped he might spill over and float down to earth with that air.

The cloud had another agenda: thunder, lightning, rain, and hail.

Inside the Cumulonimbus, the booming claps of thunder were not just deafening sounds but "unbearable physical experiences" that vibrated through Rankin's entire body.

The lightning appeared not as bolts or streaks but as a "huge, bluish sheet, several feet thick" and struck so close to him that he had the sensation he was being sliced in half.

Hail pounded Rankin like a "symphony of hammers, drumming at every part of my body." The rain was so heavy that he had to hold his breath several times for fear of drowning in midair. Rankin imagined his rescuers finding him later—hanging from some tree in his parachute harness, his lungs full of water—and wondering how on earth he could have drowned.

Eventually the air became smoother and the rain more gentle. Rankin could discern the white billows of his parachute canopy against the gray clouds. A patch of green flashed between a break in the clouds, then farm fields and woods. Rankin's parachute caught the tops of pine trees, and his body struck the trunk of one tree hard. Rankin was bruised, stunned, battered, drenched, frostbitten, and exhausted but conscious.

He looked at his watch. It was 6:40 p.m. The 47,000-foot descent—a descent that should have taken him ten minutes—had taken him forty.

Rankin found his way to a road at the edge of the field where he flagged down a ride to the nearest hospital. From the passengers in the car, he learned he was in Rich Square, North Carolina—over 70 miles from Norfolk, where he had entered the cloud. Rankin's plane crashed in a field 13 miles away and left a blackened crater where it burned and nearly vaporized. No one on the ground had been injured. Rankin suffered minor injuries—bruises, lacerations, frostbite, sprains, and strains, and a cut tendon in his little finger. He was discharged from the hospital two weeks later and was back flying just several weeks after that.

Less than a year later, Rankin encountered another thunderstorm, the first since his harrowing ordeal. It was in the middle of the night, and Rankin was in bed, half asleep, at the Armed Forces Staff College outside Norfolk. Rankin sensed stillness in the air. A flash of pale light painted his room an eerie blue. Thunder rumbled in the distance. Then came wind and rain, lightning and thunder, rattling windows, shaking walls. Rankin lay awake, testing his nerves.

"But instead of fear," he wrote, "I felt a subtle kinship to the storm, almost as if we two had some secret between us that no one else on earth could share."

Cumulonimbus

Commonly known as "thunderheads" or "storm clouds," the enormous and powerful Cumulonimbus clouds have earned nicknames such as the King of Clouds, Godfather of Clouds, Darth Vader of Clouds, and the Tyrannosaurus of the Cloud World.

During the summers on the East Coast, where I grew up, dark Cumulonimbus clouds would appear in the western sky every day—every afternoon at four o'clock, it seemed. With the first rumble of thunder, my mother would call me and my three brothers in from the yard. We'd scramble around following my mother's orders: close all the windows in the house, unplug the clothes dryer and television sets, check the car windows, draw extra water in case the power went out, find the dog, comfort the dog, make sure our bare feet weren't wet, and—when we were are all done—stay inside but do not sit in front of a window. I never questioned this last rule, which was not intended to prevent us from watching the storm but to keep us safe from the lightning that we were told might come in through the gaps around the windows. Had I been allowed to watch the "storm clouds" during my childhood thunderstorms, it might not have taken me so long to develop a kinship with them, utter their Latin name, and learn something about their marvelous fearsome selves.

Cumulonimbus is a massive cloud with a low base that can spread to several miles across and a top that can rise to 45,000 feet and beyond. Because Cumulonimbus clouds rise through all three altitude levels they are often classified separately from the low clouds and categorized as "clouds with vertical development." This impressive development is due, in part, to the tremendous amounts of energy released within the clouds—that latent heat of condensation created when water vapor condenses into liquid water. The release of this heat helps keep Cumulonimbus clouds afloat and creates powerful updrafts in them.

Well-developed Cumulus congestus are easy to confuse with Cumulonimbus. Both are towering, impressively huge clouds, and the former can morph into the latter in matter of minutes. A Cumulus congestus has a tight, cauliflower-like top. When the top of this cloud becomes fibrous and the base turns dark gray and produces strong rain shafts, it is officially a Cumulonimbus. Although there is much ice within it, the ice at the top—the ice that causes the fibrous appearance—is clearly visible when you observe these clouds on the horizon. On occasion you can also observe the icy top of a Cumulonimbus spread out horizontally in a smooth anvil shape (Cumulonimbus incus) as it reaches the boundary of the troposphere, above which the air temperature no longer decreases with increased altitude. Above the tropopause, the air warms instead of cools with increased altitude, and so the clouds can no longer rise. The tropopause marks the ceiling of most Cumulonimbus clouds, though when the updrafts within these clouds are especially strong, the tops of Cumulonimbus can cross the tropopause into the next higher layer of the atmosphere, the stratosphere.

The fibrous top and rain shafts mark the birth of a Cumulonimbus cloud and also the beginning of its dramatic deterioration, which includes heavy rain, strong winds, and often hail, thunder, and lightning. The strong updrafts within Cumulonimbus clouds also create strong downdrafts, which increase the intensity of the rainfall and hurling of hailstones to the ground.

These downdrafts inhibit the clouds' development by cutting off the supply of warm air from thermals on the ground. As the updrafts within the Cumulonimbus weaken, the moist air beneath the cloud cannot rise to condensation level. New cloud droplets do not form, and old cloud droplets begin to evaporate.

If the thunderstorm is short-lived—less than an hour—it may be the work of a single Cumulonimbus cloud. If, on the other hand, the storm rages on for hours, there may be several Cumulonimbus clouds in play as either a succession of single clouds or as a cluster of clouds. The clusters, or multicell storm complexes, are composed of individual convective clouds, each in a different stage of development. If you know where your local storms usually form, you can watch the horizon in that direction and see a complex of younger Cumulus clouds and Cumulonimbus clouds together. While the mature Cumulonimbus is actively storming, the younger Cumulus clouds are building for a succession of "one-two punch" storms.

Though I didn't know it then, these multicell storm complexes were likely what shook my childhood home for hours at a time during summer. Not until I was a young adult did I begin watching thunderstorms from outside porches—and enjoying the sound and fury of Cumulonimbus. Now that I live in the Pacific Northwest, where thunderstorms are less common, the sound of thunder has become more nostalgic than frightening, the appearance of thunderheads more an invitation than a warning.

Cloud Survey Question

 Have you ever experienced a cloud close up?

> *I was fascinated with being in a cloud . . . but disappointed when I found out that being in a cloud isn't anything like being in cotton candy or feathers or marshmallows or whatever else clouds look like. It is mostly just a dampness around you.*
> *Walking to school in the fog . . . it was always eerie when you couldn't see more than five feet in front of you.*
> *Chilly, wet, lost.*

Yes, it's one of my favorite things about flying out of SeaTac. I love how it can be gross and gray and rainy down here but as you rise up through the thick cloud layer and come out the top, it's gorgeous and sunny, and sometimes you can see the top of Mt. Rainier rising up out of the clouds.

I can't recall specifics because there was probably too much wine involved. Ha ha. Just kidding. My first memory of being in a cloud was in the winter in a meadow and we were snowmobiling and we all stopped and wondered at its magnificence and then drove through it which was very exciting and probably pretty stupid!

I climbed the only mountain peak in the Adirondacks that I have ever attempted (bad sentence). I couldn't see a thing—as in a view— thanks to the clouds. I did see the metallic marker that is conveniently placed at the summit so that you know for sure that you have arrived.

One of my favorite experiences was hiking up to the continental divide in Glacier National Park, through some little drizzly cumulus puff balls. Once above the clouds, I had the experience of looking down on a rainbow that seemed to drift up the hills toward me.

When I was little and read "Humphrey the Lost Whale." At the end of the book there was this picture of clouds super low to the ground, and when we went to San Francisco, I asked my mom if we'd see clouds like that and if I'd get to bounce on them. She said most likely not.

Early in the morning in the spring when a layer of fog forms over Puget Sound. I love rowing through clouds—one of the more amazing things in life.

I was backpacking in Mt. Rainier National Park and hiked over a wooded pass. As soon as we hit the top of the pass, we got blasted with cool air and cloud cover. It was like walking right into a wall of clouds. The temperature dropped about 20 degrees. It was amazing!

Yes—while skiing and completely unable to see and falling.

Hiking in misty conditions—really wet afterward and hair totally frizzy. Lots of moisture in them clouds.

On a mountain hike up through the cloud layer, we got very wet and even though it wasn't raining, the fir trees were dripping water. It was like they were combing the moisture out of the cloud.

Yes, when hiking in the mountains. The awesome part of that is when you actually hike through and then above the clouds and then can look at them from on high.

ATMOSPHERE

A cloud is a visible mass of water droplets or ice
*crystals suspended in the **atmosphere** above the earth.*

Early on in my study of clouds and the atmosphere, I read that Earth is surrounded by a staggering 5.5 quadrillion tons of air. That's 5,500,000,000,000,000 tons.

This came as a bit of a shock to me. Weren't weightless-seeming things "as light as air?" Didn't things vanish into "thin air" and become invisible? Wasn't air about the closest thing you could get to nothing?

Let's take those big numbers personally. Imagine a column of air one inch square in cross section, extending from sea level to the "top" of the atmosphere, which is 310 miles up. This column of air weighs nearly 14.7 pounds. The area of the top of the average person's head and shoulders is about 155 square inches, so we are all standing under a whopping 2,278.5 pounds of air. That's over a ton of air.

When I reported these findings to my husband and oldest son, they were both lying on their backs on the kitchen floor, busy stretching their hamstrings. They gave me a look. I knew this look well. It said that I was making this up, that I had probably done the math wrong by adding a few zeroes, that only someone without a science background would be alarmed by the weight of air.

"Why are we not pancaked under all this weight?" I asked.

My son ignored me. My husband muttered something about lung capacity. I took a deep breath, held it for a while. My skin felt the same, and my shoulders did not rise up to ear level. I exhaled and nothing changed. Clearly my lung capacity was irrelevant here. How do we actually withstand the crushing weight of air so blithely? How do the clouds respond to it so gracefully?

I hoisted the first volume of my OED onto my desk and began. "Atmosphere" is derived from two Greek words—*atmos*, meaning "vapor or steam," and *sphaera*, meaning "sphere." This name was not first used in ancient Greece but was invented in the seventeenth century and first appeared in print in 1638 in *The Discovery of the World in the Moone*, by John Wilkins, founding member of the Royal Society, the British national academy of science.

From a scanned digital facsimile of this discourse online, I found Wilkins's own description of the "atmo-sphaera" as "an orbe of grosse vaporous aire immediately encompassing the body of the Moone." Yes, the moon. The presence of the "atmo-sphaera" was part of Wilkins's proposition that the moon was a planet. In the context of the original definition, the term "sphaera" described not the shape of a planet but the area, or realm, of its activity—as in the "sphere of its influence." According to my OED, the word "atmosphere" was used later to describe the ring or orb of vapor thought to be "exhaled by the body of a planet."

The modern definition of atmosphere describes the gaseous mass enveloping a planet or moon. Earth's atmosphere extends from its surface to 310 miles above it, and scientists have divided it into six layers, like concentric layers of an onion, based on the temperature patterns, the presence or absence of different gasses, and the density of the gasses in each layer. Moving outward from Earth's surface, we have the troposphere, stratosphere, mesosphere, thermosphere, ionosphere, and then exosphere. Beyond the exosphere layer, the atmosphere becomes thinner and thinner as it merges with the space that surrounds all the planets in our solar system.

Where the Clouds Are

To be honest, I had never given much thought to the layers of the atmosphere. The atmosphere was just air that was "out there" between me and the stars, with the clouds somewhere in the middle. I was delighted to have the chance to explore the clouds' home territory—and mine—in a little more depth.

In reality, the troposphere and the other layers of the atmosphere are less like an onion or layer cake and more like a pile of comforters constantly and irregularly undulating as if ticklish children and puppies were squirming between them. The troposphere begins at ground level and extends to an altitude of 5 miles at the poles to 11 miles in the tropics. These natural variations in the depth of the troposphere occur not only with latitude but also according to the season and the intensity of sunlight—all of which affect the expansion of the air and conditions where clouds form.

The troposphere is rumpled and also quite thin. Relative to the size of the earth, the troposphere is comparable to the leather cover on a softball. Within this relatively thin layer we find most of the nitrogen and oxygen that make up our breathable air, all our wind and rain and snow, and nearly all of our clouds.

I say "nearly all" because two rare clouds, known as nacreous and noctilucent, occur above the troposphere. They are not species, varieties, or supplementary features, but are classified as "Special Clouds" in the new *International Cloud Atlas*.

Nacreous, or "mother of pearl" clouds, are named for their resemblance to the soft iridescent lining—the nacre—inside a mollusk shell. They form as moisture penetrates the boundary layer between the lower troposphere and the stratosphere.

Above the stratosphere, noctilucent or "night-shining" clouds occur in the mesosphere, the atmospheric layer above the stratosphere. These clouds are thin, bluish-white, and composed of tiny ice crystals. Studies have suggested that the water in these clouds may originate from meteoroids encountering the mesosphere, the first dense region of gas on their way toward Earth.

Around twilight, alert and lucky cloud watchers have observed both noctilucent and nacreous clouds from the Pacific Northwest and other high-latitude locales. Like many other cloud watchers, I have seen these clouds only in photographs. I would love to see these clouds in person—not only because they are rare and beautiful, but also because I would like to rest my eyes on a cloud so high—so deep—in our atmosphere.

Earth's atmosphere has not always been so friendly to clouds or to life as we know it.

Some 4.6 billion years ago, Earth's first atmosphere was most likely hydrogen, helium, methane, ammonia, and other gasses that escaped into space from the hot surface of the earth during its formation. This early atmosphere lacked two ingredients essential for life—oxygen and water. Gradually, gasses trapped in molten rock within Earth's hot interior escaped through volcanoes and vents to create our second atmosphere of nitrogen, hydrogen, carbon dioxide, and water vapor. Some of the water vapor remained in the atmosphere; most condensed and rained down as liquid to create our oceans and rivers. Earth's atmosphere had clouds, but not enough oxygen to sustain life.

Where did all the oxygen come from? It did not accumulate from the simple breaking down of H_2O as I guessed but instead from cyanobacteria. About three billion years ago, these microscopic, single-celled organisms photosynthesized sunlight and in the process split the water and carbon dioxide molecules and recombined them to form organic compounds and also oxygen. At first, most of the oxygen produced by the cyanobacteria never made it into the atmosphere but instead bonded with other minerals and elements in the oceans and rocks to create various oxides (such as iron oxide, or rust). Not until about six hundred million years ago did the cyanobacteria produce enough oxygen to allow for the release of oxygen into the atmosphere—and therefore for multicelled organisms, including plankton, to develop and thrive. About five hundred million years ago, during a surge in photosynthetic plankton in our oceans, oxygen production also surged. During this time, oxygen levels climbed from as low as 10 percent to as high as 28 percent, and then eventually settled at its current 22 percent.

The origin of nitrogen in our atmosphere is still something of a scientific mystery. Some theories point to Earth itself as a source, suggesting that as magma outgassed while the planet was forming, nitrogen formed from ammonia (NH_3) and other compounds. Other theories point to Jupiter as the deliverer of nitrogen-bearing ices early in its history when this outer planet may have traveled through other orbits in our solar system. Wherever this element hails from, it serves as a buffer for the reactive (and often corrosive) oxygen in our atmosphere.

Pressure

Meteorologists and weathercasters make it easy to ignore the weight of air. They refer to it as "atmospheric pressure" or "barometric pressure" and talk about "high pressure" and "low pressure" without ever referring to the weight behind the pressure—the weight of air.

Galileo proved four centuries ago that air had weight, yet I had just now become curious about this strange but universally accepted fact.

A friend told me that if you know nothing about something, start with a children's book. Which is why I ended up on my hands and knees at my public library, scanning the shelves for books on clouds, the weather, and the atmosphere. I checked out a dozen big, flat books. I kept them in a canvas bag under my desk and read them surreptitiously when no one was home. What I read confused me. What I read made me pity our youth.

"Air pressure is the force of air pressing down on the ground or any other horizontal surface."

I closed this particular book and laid it flat on the table in a horizontal position. Indeed, it stayed put. I set the book in a vertical position. It did not float up like it was on the moon. I placed the book in the reject pile.

"Atmospheric pressure is simply the weight of air. You don't feel it because the pressure is distributed in all directions and there's also air inside your body pushing outward."

How many nine-year-old boys would snicker at this one? Imagine the uproar in the classroom when the jokes began!

"Because air is a fluid, the pressure it exerts comes from all directions."

I recalled that not all fluids are liquids but failed to see the cause-and-effect logic here.

"Air pressure is the weight of the air pressing down on the earth."

Down? Had I not just read that the pressure comes from all directions?

"Pressure is a force. A force is defined as a push or a pull. In the case of air pressure, it is just a push."

Uh-huh.

"High pressure areas (or highs) are like mountains of air. That means there's more air above you. So your pressure is higher."

Nothing like a tautology to enlighten curious young minds!

"Atmospheric pressure is the weight of the atmosphere on a specific point of the Earth's surface."

A solid start, but, judging by what came next, I guessed that the author panicked when he failed to come up with a clarifying sentence or a handy metaphor and wrote this instead: "Measurement is done with a barometer and can be expressed in different units of measure, either hectoPascals (hPa) (formerly called millibars (mbar)) or millimeters of mercury (mmHg). Average pressure at sea level is 1013 hPa of 760 mmHg."

Wow.

"Think of air as a three-dimensional pool table where all the balls are moving and bumping into one another constantly. The effect of all this moving and bumping is pressure."

Aren't pool tables already three-dimensional? Did the author not mean to ask us to think of the balls moving and bumping into each other in the air *above* the flat surface of the 3-D pool table? Too bad there is not a friendly synonym for "multiplanar."

Other books explained that we don't feel air pressure because "we are used to it" or "we are structured to withstand the pressure." Who was "we" exactly? Homo sapiens? Vertebrates? Mammals? Did worms, beetles, fish, jellyfish, trees, fungus, and other "differently structured" living things feel the pressure differently?

Thinking that some hands-on learning would help me, I found instructions for making a barometer to measure air pressure at home. The only equipment I needed was a balloon and a can. Luckily, I had both that day. I stretched a purple "Happy Birthday" balloon from a kitchen drawer over an empty, well-rinsed can of black-eyed peas from my recycling bin. I set my barometer near a window because I figured that the air trapped in the can should be nearer the outside "natural" air so it could better respond to its changing pressure. Such reasoning was so tragically dim-witted that it had nowhere to go but into comedy. I chuckled every time I saw my barometer. Which is why I did not move the can for the next two weeks.

The balloon bulged and slumped slightly during this time. Every time I checked the can, I'd look out the window. What was happening on the three-inch-wide surface of the balloon may have been in sync with the barometric pressure, but it seemed out of sync with what the clouds were doing. When I thought I heard the clouds snickering, I threw out the balloon and recycled the can.

Jell-O

"How are your clouds?" a friend asked.

I groaned.

"I don't get atmospheric pressure. It just doesn't make sense."

Her eyes lit up. "I can explain this! I am really good at explaining science! Oh, boy! This is great!"

We had just been out to breakfast together and were standing on the side of the road by our parked cars, keys in hand, ready to depart. My friend, a retired scientist, launched in anyway.

"Okay. What happens when you take a bag of potato chips on an airplane?"

"I eat them."

"No!"

"My husband eats them?"

"I'm serious. What happens?"

She did not wait for me to answer.

"The bag expands!" my friend shouted, as if that explained everything.

It did not. A car pulled up, ready to take my parking space, but I waved the driver on.

"Because you're flying at a high altitude and the air pressure is lower," she continued, "the air in the bag can expand because there is no pressure against the air inside the bag."

"So—"

"So imagine the cells in your body are little bags of potato chips, pressing against the pressure of the atmosphere."

"I'm sorry, but I can't do that."

She was disappointed but not daunted.

"I cannot imagine my cells are little bags of potato chips," I said. "The sharp corners of the little bags hurt. I need another metaphor. Whatever you do, do not say that the atmosphere is 'like an ocean of air, and we live at the bottom of it' like all the books I read tell me—because when I am swimming in the ocean I float at the top. I cannot get to the bottom of the ocean without wearing cement shoes and having my lungs fill up with water. The atmosphere as an ocean ruins the ocean for me. In fact, I'm feeling a little claustrophobic just thinking about it."

"How about Jell-O?" she asked. "Can you imagine the atmosphere like Jell-O—surrounding you on all sides, putting pressure on all sides of your body equally?"

Yes. Yes, in fact, I *could* imagine myself in a swimming pool filled with blue Jell-O. I could feel the pressure from all sides. Then a green grape appeared in my atmosphere. The kind of skinless pale-green grape that comes in fruit cocktail. The fruit cocktail my mother used to mix into Jell-O to make it "healthy." And then I remembered the other fruits—slimy cubes of peaches, pallid cubes of pear, a stingy number of maraschino cherries. All this fruit was suspended in my blue Jell-O atmosphere.

I was no longer listening to my friend. She noticed.

"I was thinking about fruit cocktail," I confessed.

"You know what you need?" she asked. "You need to rent that movie with Temple Grandin—you know, the brilliant woman with autism. It's called *Thinking in Pictures*. You think differently."

Unable to think of a response, I let it go. I was happy that—despite the bits of fruit—this sensation of Jell-O on my skin was not unlike atmospheric pressure. I was one step closer to the clouds.

Two-Wheeling in the Atmosphere

My scientist friend and I planned to have another conversation about pressure during a bike ride on a stretch of the Chehalis Western Trail near her home. It was a mild October morning, the sky covered by thin Altostratus, with rain in the forecast. When we met up at her house, my friend was wearing a high-visibility yellow-green jacket, black sweat pants, and sports sandals. Under the sandals, socks. Over the socks, bread bags. She had a blister, she explained, and couldn't wear sneakers. She wore a clear shower cap to keep her hair dry and a pink flowery chiffon scarf, tied under her chin, to protect her ears from the wind. Over the scarf, her bike helmet. She looked like a mad scientist on a bike, but not like Einstein. We set off, and she called out the turns on the rural roads leading to the trail as we talked.

"I'm going to start at the beginning," she announced. "Most of the weight of air comes from the weight of nitrogen and oxygen."

She was speaking to me as if I were in sixth grade. Which was perfect.

"That weight is derived from the mass—the amount of matter—in each atom of each molecule. That matter is the protons, neutrons, and electrons in each atom. But it's mostly the proton and neutron, which have almost the same mass; the electron is about two thousand times lighter than either so it hardly counts. Turn left here."

We were on a curving, shoulderless road, biking single file. She was in the lead and shouting.

"The mass of a single atom is unimaginably small and is measured in AMUs."

"In what?"

"AMUs," she repeated, enunciating each letter. "Atomic Mass Units."

"One AMU is 1.66×10^{-24} grams. Turn right here."

"I can't even think of such a tiny number," I said.

We turned onto the bike trail, which was wide enough to bike side by side. I was grateful that the trail was flat. I couldn't have handled hills and a steep learning curve at the same time.

"Don't worry about the number. Just remember that the heaviest atom, uranium, has mass of 238 AMU and the lightest, hydrogen, is just over 1 AMU. Helium is just over 4."

"Where do nitrogen and oxygen weigh in?" I asked.

"Nitrogen is about 14 and oxygen 16. But remember, in the atmosphere, nitrogen and oxygen always come in bonded pairs—N_2 and O_2—so you double it to get their molecular weight, 28 and 32 respectively."

"So only hydrogen and helium are actually lighter than air?" I asked.

"Those two and a few more, but don't worry about that."

"Fine."

"You know that mass is not the same as weight, right?"

"Yup."

I must not have sounded convincing.

"People use 'mass' and 'weight' as if they were the same but they aren't," my friend said. "Mass is constant, weight fluctuates. Weight is the measurement of the force of gravity on the mass of an object. Keep straight here."

"Gravity is the strong, invisible force pulling everything—including the air—down toward Earth. As the nitrogen and oxygen molecules are pulled downward, they are squeezed closer together. The closer the molecules are to Earth, the more they are squeezed by the weight of the molecules above them. We need to go single file here."

We crossed over a highway on a bridge. The traffic was loud, and my friend stopped talking. I had less than a minute to think.

"Can you tell me about the difference between low and high pressure?" I asked when we got to the other side. "I did an experiment with a balloon and an empty can, and it made no sense."

"Let me guess. The balloon bulged when the outside pressure was low and the balloon slumped when the pressure was high. Turn right, here."

"I'm not sure," I admitted. "There were clouds in the sky whether it was bulging or slumping."

"Well, then. If the atmospheric pressure is low, that means the weight of the air is light. Clouds can form because air can rise to condensation level. If the atmospheric pressure is high, the weight is heavier and basically suppresses cloud development."

"Temperature differences make pressure differences and pressure differences drive winds," I said in a pedantic voice.

"What?" my friend asked.

"It's the only thing I remember from a DVD lecture on meteorology."

"Do you know what it means?"

"Not really. I've obviously memorized it. I hoped it would make sense one day."

"Today is your lucky day. Atmospheric pressure changes because the temperature of the air changes. Air temperatures change because the sun doesn't strike the planet equally, and the planet doesn't warm and cool equally. Right?"

"Right. We have night and day, seasons, deserts, oceans, and—"

"So temperature differences make pressure differences, and pressure differences drive winds, but, more importantly for you, the pressure differences drive cloud variety. Temperature and pressure are always changing. That's why the clouds are always changing."

"It seems kind of simple when you put it that way."

"Good."

She suggested we take a short break from our conversation so we could fully appreciate the scenery—a long stretch of bigleaf maples in their bright autumn yellow against the gray sky, the farm pond, horses grazing in a pasture. I gave it thirty seconds and then launched back in.

"Why does 'low' mean 'light' and 'high' mean 'heavy?'"

"I'm not sure if you're asking these questions because you're really smart or really stupid," she asked.

"The former," I snapped.

"I'm not so sure."

"Think about it," I said. "When we talk about air pressure, 'low' means 'light' and 'high' means 'heavy.' When we talk about clouds, 'low' and 'high' refer to altitude of their bases. Some high clouds, Cirrus, form under low pressure. Some low clouds, such as Stratus and Cumulus humilis, form under high pressure. Look at Cumulus humilis, for instance, the cloud know as the 'fairweather Cumulus.' These are low clouds that form from thermals rising strongly from the ground during fair weather when the pressure is high. You'll see these little clouds on gorgeous blue-sky days."

"Huh. I see your point. And air pressure *lowers* as your altitude gets higher."

"Maybe you can tell me," I said, "why human beings are not crushed under the 14.7 pounds per square inch of atmospheric pressure."

"That's easy! Air exerts pressure downward and also in all directions. Think about all those air molecules zinging around every which way. You hear about 14.7 pounds per square inch, but not the other pressure coming from different directions. And all the molecules in your body are exerting pressure too. People don't talk about it because you don't usually feel any imbalance except when you are flying, and your ears pop. That's your body equalizing the pressure. Did I ever tell you about biking with my friend and her daughter?"

She did not wait for a reply.

"So, one time I went on a bike ride with a friend and her daughter. In no time, my friend and I were way ahead of the daughter. She wasn't particularly fit, and she had a pretty clunky bike. When I circled around to see if there was some problem, I noticed her tires were really low. When I told her, she said, 'I know. I let the air out of them so they would be lighter and I could keep up.'"

I burst out laughing.

My friend smiled, relieved.

Clouds on Other Planets

While I was studying Earth's atmosphere, my youngest son came home from his first semester in college and sent me back to kindergarten. We were sitting around the kitchen table talking about his classes when he asked, innocently enough, "So, are you going to write about clouds on other planets?"

I wasn't aware that there were clouds on other planets. But I didn't tell him that. I told him that I had my hands full with Earth's clouds.

"And even if there *were* clouds on other planets," I said, a bit dismissively, "they wouldn't be our kind of clouds—watery, life-sustaining, Earth clouds. You know—*clouds*."

My son called my bluff. He left the room and came back with *The Essential Cosmic Perspective*, his Astronomy 101 textbook. He opened the book to an illustration showing three distinct cloud layers on Jupiter, set the book down in front of me, and then headed off to meet his friends.

My son was right. There are clouds on other planets. But I was right too. They are not like Earth's clouds.

I started with the Jovian planets—Neptune, Uranus, Saturn, and Jupiter—also known as the "gas giants" because they lack a solid surface. The bright oranges, reds, and blues that make these planets so strikingly beautiful are caused in large part by clouds—thick, swirling clouds of gasses. The icy clouds on these planets occur in layers and are composed of water, ammonium hydrosulfide, ammonia, and methane. If any liquid-water clouds exist on these planets, they are buried too deep in their icy atmospheres of hydrogen, helium, and methane to see. What we *can* see of Uranus and Neptune are their stunning blue colors, caused by clouds of methane snowflakes, which reflect the sun's blue light back to space.

Saturn has three layers of ice clouds, together about 124 miles thick. These ice clouds are composed of ammonia, a mix of ammonia hydrosulfide and water (ice), and ammonia mixed with water (droplets)—nothing you would want to breathe or have rain down you.

When my husband walked into the kitchen, I explained to him what I was reading and why.

"Don't forget to look at Titan," he said. "I think they've just discovered some strange clouds there."

Now, under pressure from both Dr. Science and Dr. Science Jr., I went off for a brief visit to Titan via the internet.

On Titan, one of Saturn's fifty moons, NASA scientists discovered in 2016 a seemingly "impossible" type of ice cloud made of a compound of carbon and nitrogen known as dicyanoacetylene. What puzzled scientists was that there didn't seem to be enough of this compound (just 1 percent) in Titan's stratosphere to condense into clouds. Scientists estimated that the clouds should need at least one hundred times more dicyanoacetylene vapor to produce the ice clouds they were observing. The current theory is that these clouds form through chemical reactions between ice particles and other compounds—reactions that are triggered by ultraviolet light. A similar process occurs in Earth's stratosphere when chlorine compounds attach to ice crystals, and ultraviolet light from the sun triggers a reaction that produces chlorine—a gas that contributes to the depletion of the ozone layer over Earth's poles.

I returned to reading my son's textbook, half dreading more examples of ways our clouds could turn on us and become toxic, full of chlorine or methane, or too thin, thick, or cold to protect us.

The clouds on Jupiter, the closest gas giant to Earth, are about 62 miles thick and occur in three separate layers. The inner layer of whitish-gray clouds formed in nearly Earth-like temperatures from condensed water. Covering these clouds is a middle layer of ammonium hydrosulfide clouds that reflect red and brown light. And covering these are whitish-yellow clouds of condensed ammonia.

Was my throat burning and eyes stinging or was it just my imagination?

I bid the gas giants farewell and landed on the solid-surface planets, the first being Mars, which has no clouds whatsoever and a very thin atmosphere of carbon dioxide. Mars's surface temperature is too cold for liquid water, but scientists theorize that some three billion years ago, liquid water may have been present on this planet as is evidenced by features such as river beds and floodplains apparently carved by water. Much of the water vapor once present on Mars may have been stripped away by the solar wind.

The atmosphere on Venus is 99 percent carbon dioxide and has an atmospheric pressure of 1,323 pounds per square inch—ninety times Earth's pressure. Standing on Venus would feel to us like standing about a half mile under the ocean. Nitrogen and water make up the remaining 1 percent of the Venutian atmosphere—not enough to make watery, welcoming clouds. The thick and turbulent layer of clouds that completely hide the surface of Venus are composed of carbon dioxide and tinged with sulfuric acid. I have seen this planet twinkling in the night sky many times, but I never imagined I was looking at its clouds.

Mercury, the planet closest to the sun, has a tenuous atmosphere composed of nearly half oxygen and half sodium, helium, and potassium. Scientists have detected the presence of water vapor too, which may have originated from comets or deep craters in the planet's dark, cold polar regions. Without a blanket of clouds to moderate its surface temperature, Mercury can swing from 800°F during the day and plummet to −280°F at night. It is extremely inhospitable to life.

My virtual planetary cloud tour left me exhausted and in need of some fresh air. It was close to dusk on this dreary December day, so I bundled up and took a brisk walk around the neighborhood. The air was cold, but every breath felt good. The widespread layer of Altostratus dimmed any possibility of a glimpse of the setting sun. No matter. I felt a deepened sense of gratitude for these and all of Earth's benign and beneficial clouds and for its life-giving atmosphere with its just-right mix of nitrogen and oxygen, its rumpled layers, its impossibly huge and impossibly small weights, its lows and highs, its bulges and slumps—all of it.

Stratocumulus

Clouds play a critical and complex role in maintaining the just-right temperature range of Earth and its atmosphere. They are capable of cooling our planet by scattering incoming infrared radiation (the sun's energy that we feel as warmth but cannot see) back to space and by reemitting outgoing infrared radiation (the heat absorbed and then released at the earth's surface.) Clouds can also warm the planet by trapping the outgoing infrared radiation. In light of warming temperatures associated with climate change, the low, lumpy, layered Stratocumulus play an inordinately important role as Earth's thermostat.

Stratocumulus occur in the low range of low altitudes—generally between 2,000 and 6,500 feet. Low clouds tend to be thicker than high clouds, and thicker clouds tend to reflect more incoming infrared radiation than thin clouds. Stratocumulus aren't particularly thick clouds, however. They block more infrared radiation from reaching Earth's surface because they are so abundant. In fact, more of Earth's surface is covered by Stratocumulus than any other type of cloud. Scientists estimate that these clouds cover 23 percent of Earth's ocean surface and 12 percent of its landmasses. An estimated 80 percent of Stratocumulus clouds occur over oceans, and we get our fair share of these clouds in the Pacific Northwest as they push inland from the Pacific Ocean to our coasts. They comprise an especially varied cloud genus and are sometimes hard to distinguish from certain species of Stratus and Cumulus clouds.

One of the best ways to see the distinctive features of Stratocumulus clouds is from satellite imagery, which shows them as vast layers of small rolls or bands of rolls, often closely fitted together in a repeating pattern with no overlap or gaps. So beautiful are these tessellations that I found it easier to see them as art than as hardworking thermostats for our atmosphere.

I had a chance to observe these clouds in person one April afternoon as they drifted in from the Pacific Ocean. I was not expecting to see them, nor was I prepared for the magic they brought inland.

The Cloud Forest

Early on in my study of clouds, I had planned to study the ten types by traveling across the entire state of Washington. I studied the climate, topography, flora, landforms, and weather patterns of our state's ten distinct bioregions, and laid out an ambitious plan to make ten separate trips, each to coincide with the appearance of one particular cloud type. To my knowledge, no one had studied the clouds this way so I was excited about my novel approach. What better way to kick off my cloud tour than with a Nimbostratus immersion weekend in the rain forest in April? You know April, as in April showers.

Olympia is within a few hours of the four temperate rain forests within Olympic National Park. Each rain forest lies in a river valley that channels moisture in from the Pacific Ocean. The Quinault Rain Forest, the one closest to my home, receives an average of 144 inches of precipitation a year, most of it in the form of rain, all of it brought by the clouds.

With a foul-weather friend and suitcase full of raingear, I set off for the Quinault one April morning. The temperature wasn't much over 45°F, and the sky was gray with Nimbostratus, but we didn't mind the prospect of cold, drenching hikes by day as long as we had the comforts of the Lake Quinault Lodge by night.

Not an hour west of Olympia, however, the low clouds brightened and loosened up. Five minutes later, we were driving under blue skies. I had mistaken Stratus, the "morning fog" cloud, for Nimbostratus, the rain cloud. Perhaps, I told my friend hopefully, the weather in the rain forest would be different. It was not.

"It's been rainy all week," a clerk said when we checked in at the lakeside lodge. "This is the first sun we've seen in a while."

She was really cheery.

I was tempted to ask for a refund.

I decided to make the best of it and find the silver lining in this cloud. Even if it wasn't actively raining, I could experience the legacy of the clouds—the thousand-year-old evergreens, the shoulder-high sword ferns, the pillowy tapestry of mosses, the perpetual green twilight in the dense forests. That was my intention. On our first hike I spent most of my time gawking at the blue sky, taking photos straight up through the canopy, and saying over and over, "Can you believe this sky?"

I hoped Nimbostratus would make an appearance the next morning, but when I peeked out of the curtains, I saw blue sky and spectacular clouds. Was this not Nimbostratus season in the rain forest? What were these lofty, scallop-edged Cumulus clouds doing here? I should have been thrilled, but it had taken months to plan my cloud tour. The least the clouds could do was cooperate.

"I am not getting out of bed until it starts raining," I announced to my friend. I made a cup of tea, lolled around, flipped through a field guide, and worked on my attitude. At nine o'clock, I abandoned hope, and my friend and I set out for another spectacular fair-weather hike.

Later that afternoon, I walked down to the south shore of Lake Quinault. The sky was blue above me, but a band of low clouds was moving inland along the north side of the lake. I stood and watched them. The clouds churned energetically, and I guessed they were freshly formed over the Pacific Ocean 30 miles to the west. They cast deep shadows on the forested green hills and turned the lake a chilling blackish gray. Were these clouds Stratus, Stratocumulus, or Cumulus? I couldn't tell. Whatever they were, they looked like they had an agenda.

They did, but it wasn't the rain I wanted.

These clouds had something more spectacular in mind.

The lowest clouds grazed the tops of the hills, softened at their bases, and appeared to lower themselves into the trees below the ridgeline. The hills took on a misty and diaphanous look as if they were being draped in a very thin, sheer white curtain. Or being visited by a ghost. The clouds seemed to be going out of focus, letting go of any sense of their edges, as soft and ragged as they were. These clouds were falling apart before my eyes. They were beautiful in their un-becoming.

I watched a long while, trying to figure out what was going on. Were trees passively combing moisture from the clouds? Were the clouds gently raining? Was there a minimum distance a drop of water had to fall to be considered rain? Or was this snow? It was well above freezing where I stood, but as one cloud rose up over the highest peak, the evergreens near the top of the windward flank turned white. Was it a dusting of snow—a restrained shake of confectioner's sugar through a sifter? Or was it frozen fog? Or something else?

When I returned home, I sent my meteorologist a few photographs with my usual, "What's going on here?" subject line. He guessed they were Stratus but would need the date, time, and location and more pictures to be certain. I sent more photos, along with the elevation of the hill above the lake: 2,600 feet. He checked the records and local temperature, freezing level, and wind direction and then deemed them Stratocumulus—ones mutating to Cumulus. Based on an estimate of the air temperature where I was standing, he calculated that the hilltop was cold enough for a snow shower.

I had never thought about Stratocumulus as a cloud that snowed. My meteorologist told me that most clouds can produce some kind of actual ground-touching drizzle, rain, snow, hail, or other kinds of precipitation. Only the high clouds—Cirrus, Cirrostratus, and Cirrocumulus—and Altocumulus clouds are "dry."

Although my plans for a Nimbostratus rain forest expedition were thwarted, I was thrilled by my serendipitous Stratocumulus snow. No matter where I encountered them, the clouds were always more capable and creative than I gave them credit for.

ABOVE

A cloud is a visible mass of water droplets or ice
*crystals suspended in the atmosphere **above** the earth.*

That a cloud is above the earth seems too obvious to state. Certainly "on top of" or "over" might have been contenders, but "a cloud on top of the earth" conjures up an image of an enormous cap cloud on the North Pole. "Over the earth" makes the clouds seem like vanilla frosting you'd spread over a cake.

"Above" best describes the cloud's position relative to the earth.

"Above" is a soft-sounding word, and it floats when you say it out loud.

The problems with this preposition start when you ask how high above the earth the clouds are. The answers are not at all obvious. At my latitude in Olympia, 47.04° N, the troposphere is about 8 miles thick. That's a lot of space—a lot of vertical space without any kind of signposts, landmarks, or visual clues to mark the distance between me and the clouds.

Developing a sense of cloud heights is not an innate skill. Not even professional, sky-watching meteorologists can point to a cloud and say for certain, "That one is 16,500 feet." If they do, it's because they have measured the cloud heights with LIDAR or a ceilometer, or they have found this information online. Or they are just making stuff up.

Knowing the elevations of the hills, mountains, water towers, skyscrapers, or other high points around you will help you with the altitudes of some of the clouds. Although I don't have a clear view of Mount Rainier from my neighborhood, this prominent snow-covered peak is visible from many places in and around Olympia, where it serves as a 14,411-foot-high measuring stick for certain clouds. Halfway up the mountain is 7,205 feet—just over the official 6,500-foot-mark between low and mid-level clouds. Clouds below the halfway mark are generally low clouds; clouds with their bases above this mark are generally mid-level. Clouds that float above the summit and seemingly behind it are mid-level or high.

For me, judging the height of a cloud's base, the depth of its vertical extent proved to be one of the most challenging aspects of cloud watching. I get more pleasure from trying to feel the depth of the atmosphere than I do from knowing the vertical distances that mark this depth. To be quite honest, vertical distances aren't my only problem. Judging horizontal distances is also challenging for me unless I am looking at a football field. The good news and the bad news is that I am not alone.

Judging Distances

One winter I signed up for a wilderness skills course offered by the Olympia Branch of The Mountaineers. The lecture on backcountry navigation included how to use a compass, how to tell the difference between small-scale and large-scale topographic maps, and how to read contour lines on those maps. The instructor had a lot of material to get through in the three-hour class and he moved apace.

Contour lines, he explained, are the concentric lines printed on maps to indicate the elevation of the land above sea level. Depending on the scale of the map, each line indicates an elevation change of 40, 80, 200, or 250 feet. Backcountry hikers and climbers prefer maps with 40-foot contour lines because they offer more—and often critical—details about the terrain. But he warned us that such a map could "hide a sheer 20-foot vertical rock wall" between two lines.

Until this point, the seventy-five students in the class had been listening attentively, taking notes, and nodding along. I began hearing whispering from the back of the classroom and grumbling from the front. A hand shot up.

"I'm a little lost here," the student began. "How can the contour lines be different distances apart if the scale of the map is the same?"

The instructor explained that the distance between the lines indicates vertical distance, not the horizontal distance. On a map with 40-foot contour intervals, the elevation changes by 40 feet between adjacent lines. The scale of the map indicates the distance you have to walk from one line to the next. On any scale map, lines very close together indicate steep terrain, lines far apart mean more gentle terrain, and—

"Okay," the student interrupted, "but what does 40 feet even *look* like?"

Calibrating the Clouds

For the most precise altitudes of the clouds near you, consult the National Weather Service's online data by going to www.weather.gov and entering your zip code for "local forecast." This will take you to current conditions and extended forecast where you'll get a snapshot of the weather, some cute visuals, but no data on the clouds. For that, look to the right side of your screen and to "More Information" and click "3 Day History." Now we are talkin' data—twenty columns of it, updated hourly, including a prominent column labeled "Clouds." This is where you'll find those codes for the clouds (BKN, SCT, FEW, OVC) followed by three numbers—BKN060, for instance. Add two zeroes to the end of the number and you have the altitude, in feet, of the clouds: the bases of these broken clouds are 6,000 feet above the ground. You now know your cloud is low and broken and so most likely Cumulus or Stratocumulus.

Unfortunately for cloud watchers, these data tables often exclude clouds above 12,000 feet—thus some mid-level clouds and all the high clouds. Our federal government meteorologists aren't ignoring these clouds entirely, but this altitude marks the limit of many automated cloud-detecting technologies installed at weather-observation stations (generally at airports).

So though you may be looking at a sky full of Altocumulus clouds, you might see the code for clear (CLR) because these clouds are over 12,000 feet. My meteorologist tells me that if there are human weather observers on staff (which is often the case at the country's larger airports), satellite imagery can be analyzed to provide more information on clouds above 12,000 feet. It is at these larger airports where the code SKC—"sky clear"—is used to indicate that there are no clouds at all at any altitude. So weather observers at LAX airport in Los Angeles can report truly clear skies (SKC), but at Olympia's small airport our skies are rarely, if ever, reported as SKC. It's not necessarily because our skies usually have clouds above 12,000 feet. It's because there's no one there to look.

Cirrocumulus

The clouds I love best are the ones that appear in Olympia most often—the Stratus clouds, the ones that sneak into my backyard, the ones I can walk and swim in. The ones I love the least are Cirrocumulus. Least not because they are unlovable but because they don't put in the time to be loved. They are often obscured by the more common lower clouds in my region. And when the do appear, they are ephemeral, discrete, and discreet.

Cirrocumulus clouds are composed almost entirely of supercooled droplets and appear as petite white cloudlets tightly packed together or laid out in rippling rows. The cloudlets are often compared to grains of rice to distinguish them from larger Altocumulus cloudlets. The "Cirro" part leads us to think this is strictly a high cloud, but Cirrocumulus clouds can also occur at mid-level too—and with such fine granulations that it's easy to believe they are much higher.

Cirrocumulus clouds cover only a small patch of the sky. If your view does not include this patch, you can easily miss them. You have to look around. When you spot some, don't take your eyes off them. If they form from ice crystals, they disintegrate almost immediately. If the supercooled droplets in these clouds remain supercooled, they will evaporate within about ten minutes. Cirrocumulus are even more ephemeral if the supercooled droplets freeze instantly after the cloudlets appear (which is often the case). You will see ice crystals falling from the cloudlets within about five minutes, and your Cirrocumulus clouds are now wispy, icy Cirrus.

Though Cirrocumulus may be uncommon and transient where I live, most people are familiar with the form that appears in an undulating layer known officially as Cirrocumulus stratiformis undulatus. Many people know this cloud formation as "mackerel skies," so named because of its resemblance to the scaly skin of this fish. Why mackerel and not cod, herring, or other scaled fish? I cannot imagine that the scales of a mackerel mimic Cirrocumulus clouds better than the scales of most other fish do. Perhaps mackerel was the most abundant commonly known fish when this cloud was first described. "Mackerel skies" is certainly more poetic sounding than "cod skies" and less fearsome than "barracuda skies," the way "mare's tails" is more poetic than "donkey tails" and less fearsome than "stallion tails."

And what makes this type of Cirrocumulus resemble fish scales? The individual water-droplet clouds are packed tightly together but are distinct, owing to the margin of blue sky around each element or cloudlet. When these clouds first form, they may be more smooth than rippled. That smoothness turns into cloudlets as the latent heat of condensation enhances the upward motion of the cloud. That upward motion is balanced by a downward motion, which leads to evaporation. This creates the cloudlets—the "scales."

When fishing for mackerel skies, pay attention. You don't want this cloud to be the one that got away.

Below

Trout, bass, and perch but no mackerel swim in Lake Saint Clair, a 233-acre lake in Thurston County, ten miles east of my home. One mid-September day, I was out on the lake with a friend to canoe to one of its many coves for a swim. After morning fog, the sun blazed in a cloudless sky. The lake was placid and quiet. A few men fished from small skiffs; one woman paddled her stand-up board around. School was back in session, and the houses around the lake looked closed up for the season—window shades were drawn, folding chairs stowed away, inflatable rafts and toys cleared off the docks. Rope swings hung forlornly from the stout branches of bigleaf maples along the shoreline. The whole place had an end-of-summer calm that put me in a wistful mood.

I had planned to tell my friend about ice, crystals, contrails, and mackerel skies, but as we paddled toward the cove, I forgot about the clouds. My friend and I talked about being mothers, daughters, and wives. From the bow, I scanned the surface of the lake and just below it for snags. I noticed, as if for the first time, how the refraction of sunlight made my wooden paddle appear to break at the surface of the water. I watched the ripples from my paddle work their way away from the canoe. I thought about wavelengths of light emanating from them. We talked about our kids, travel, home-improvement projects, and books we were reading. I wondered about the molecules of liquid water in the lake and the water vapor just above it.

Beyond the ripples of my paddle and just about twenty feet away, a patch of tiny waves ruffled the smooth water. The crest and troughs of the waves caught the light just so, and the patch brightened white against the dark lake. It looked like a Cirrocumulus cloud shimmering on the surface. Though the lake held the reflection of the sky, this cloud was not a reflection. It was just lake water moved by a breeze, a thermal, or perhaps a large school of very tiny fish. I recalled the description of Cirrocumulus from my *Guide to the Sky* poster: "When this high cloud forms, it can give the sky the appearance of wind blowing on a pond of white water."

Whatever forces caused my cloud suddenly stopped causing it. The ripples flattened, and the lake was smooth again. The wind did not kick up, no clouds developed. I scanned the surface for another ruffling as we paddled but saw none. Which made the fleeting sight more precious and memorable.

I don't see Cirrocumulus clouds very often. But when I do, I always think of that day in September and the lake that was the sky and wind that was the cloud.

Floating

I celebrated Labor Day one year by trying to fall asleep in my hammock on my back deck. The morning's layers of Stratus were hinting at leaving, so I closed my eyes and tried to drift off while they floated past.

I drifted for an hour or so but did not sleep. I deepened my breathing and opened and closed my eyes in the slowest, laziest way possible. The shade shifted, and the sun warmed my feet. A cool breezed passed over my toes and then stirred the wind chimes hanging nearby.

A line from *Second Harvest*, a translation of a dreamy little book written in 1930 by French author Jean Giono, came to mind: "He had stretched out his bare feet in the warmth and was amusing himself by wiggling his toes."

I wiggled my toes.

I opened my eyes.

The universe became very, very small.

A big-bodied dragonfly flew toward the end of my hammock, stopped, and then hovered as if trying to make sense of the bigger body newly in its flight path. The dragonfly darted toward the edge of the yard, hovered again, made a U-turn, and zipped back to my hammock as if it had forgotten something. It continued back and forth this way, flying lower with each pass until—for no reason I could think of—it flew out of the yard and up into the bright sky. Where I lost the dragonfly, an opening in the Stratus revealed a blue sky and brighter clouds above—Altocumulus, I guessed. I felt as if I was looking through a window into the sky. It was strangely disorienting.

The window closed. I shut my eyes and listened to the chickadees and nuthatches at the feeder and to a lone bee on the potted red geraniums nearby. When I felt the sun on my eyelids again, I opened my eyes. Above the parting Stratus clouds there were the Altocumulus and now some higher, brighter, clouds—the Cirrocumulus. It was all I could do to stay there in my hammock and not run inside for my polarized sunglasses, my camera, or my husband to come out and look. If I took my eyes off these elusive and ephemeral clouds, they'd be gone.

I let my eyes travel from one level of cloud to another, in and out of the sky. I noticed how my eyes felt resting on each cloud—low, middle, high. The clouds were all so different—shaded and fast, bright and slow, delicate and aloof.

I knew these clouds were floating over each other in their separate altitude levels, but I still had to work to override the illusion that they were layered close together on an imaginary celestial dome overhead. I could feel the small muscles in my eyes adjusting, the neurons behind my eyes sparkling, my brain sensing the depth of the sky in a deep and fluid way.

As the low clouds swept past, more of the sky turned blue. I turned my head away. I began counting the shades of green in the waxy-leaved shrubs a few feet away. One bright leaf facing the sun held the full silhouette of a resting grasshopper or cricket. I closed my eyes again.

Spots of light danced on the inside of my eyelids. I felt a breeze, and then something touched my bare shoulder. I opened my eyes. It was a small, tan Douglas-fir needle. I looked up to see a flurry of them falling like snow from the tree.

I wiggled my toes. Shade had fallen across the end of the hammock. I changed my position to keep my feet in the sun. The wind chimes played three of their six notes. I looked back toward my clouds. The Altocumulus had shifted, the Cirrocumulus had already begun trailing ice crystals.

Floating there, drowsy, in the late summer sun, I could not tell if the clouds were lowering or if I was rising toward them. They were freezing, melting, dissolving, evaporating. Depth and height had no place here. The miles of atmosphere between the clouds seemed like mere inches. There was nothing between the clouds and me.

Nothing below.

Nothing above.

EARTH

*A cloud is a visible mass of water droplets or ice crystals suspended in the atmosphere above the **earth**.*

In the context of clouds, "the earth" refers not just to the soil, rocks, and sand but to the whole planet—Earth—water included.

"Earth" is a strange word. It is related to the Old Frisian words *irthe*, *erthe*, and *erde*. Old Frisian, really? This is a West Germanic language spoken between the eighth and sixteenth centuries on the coast of the North Sea. It is one of the many Old Teutonic languages from which Norwegian, Danish, Swedish, Icelandic, German, English, and many other languages developed.

The etymology of "earth" is so complex, the senses and sub-senses so numerous, and the cognates so few that the editors of my *Oxford English Dictionary* seem to have thrown up their hands during the compilation of this seven-column-long entry.

"Notions of the shape and position of the earth," they write, "have so greatly changed since Old Teutonic times, while the language of the older notions has long outlived them, that it is very difficult to arrange the senses and applications of the word in any historical order. The following arrangement does not pretend to follow the development of ideas."

That the history of the word "earth" is perhaps as unknowable and chaotic as the history of Earth itself pleased me in a perverse way. As did the notion that the clouds, which thrive on Earth's chaos, might be essentially unknowable to atmospheric physicists and cloud watchers alike.

The Sphere of Influence

I usually think of clouds as being in the atmosphere above the earth so I have to remind myself that they are also *of* the earth. Our planet is nearly spherical, cockeyed, mostly covered in water, and rough. These physical features contribute to the irregular pattern of heating across the earth's surface, which, in turn, exerts a huge influence on clouds.

Earth's spherical shape means the sun does not strike the planet's surface evenly across all latitudes. In other words, the angle of incidence varies so that sunlight strikes equatorial and tropical regions at a more perpendicular angle and polar regions at an oblique angle. (Dr. Science and I recommend shining a flashlight on a grapefruit to help visualize this phenomenon.) This uneven heating causes temperature differences at the surface, which cause pressure differences in the atmosphere. The clouds are at the mercy of both temperature and pressure.

The uneven heating of the earth from pole to pole is compounded by the fact that it makes a complete rotation every twenty-four hours. This exposes the earth's surface to alternating periods of sunlight and darkness, heating and cooling.

These are not regular twelve-hours-on, twelve-hours-off periods because our planet's axis is tilted 23.5 degrees from perpendicular and because its orbit around the sun is elliptical. Over the course of a year, tilt contributes to wild swings in the duration of night and day at different latitudes. In Olympia, for example, the periods of daylight vary between eight and a half hours at winter solstice to nearly sixteen at summer solstice. At the poles, periods of daylight vary from zero to twenty-four hours. Of course, the clouds are not watching the clock or calendar but responding to the temperature and pressure changes in their own time.

Clouds also respond to the earth's surface, which is not smooth but roughened by valleys and mountains that range from 1,410 feet below sea level at the surface of the Dead Sea to 29,035 feet above it at Mount Everest. Clouds form in valleys overnight and may get trapped there for days. They evaporate in "rain shadows" in mountain lees. They follow river valleys upstream. They form as they rise over mountain barriers and rain themselves out before they descend on the leeward side. They ride oscillating waves of air downwind of mountain peaks or cling to snowy peaks.

The earth's forests, deserts, wetlands, lakes, oceans, glaciers, tundra, cities, paved surfaces, and plowed farm fields all absorb and reemit the sun's energy at different rates and in different amounts. This affects the surface temperatures of the earth. Clouds notice this, and while they are clinging to the spinning, orbiting, tilted, sun-dappled Earth, they are reacting to these features as well. Their nimbleness is dizzying.

Of all the earth's physical features, the oceans exert perhaps the largest influence on the clouds. Covering 71 percent of the globe, oceans are the primary source of the water necessary for the formation of clouds. Each year, about 80,000 cubic miles of water are evaporated from our oceans by the sun. In comparison, only 15,000 cubic miles of water are evaporated over land surfaces. Mixed in with all that water evaporating from the ocean are the salt, minerals, phytoplankton, and other particles that serve as cloud condensation nuclei or ice nuclei.

Oceans both absorb and reflect solar radiation but are much slower to warm and cool than the land surfaces on Earth. The Pacific Ocean off the Pacific Northwest coast typically ranges from a chilly 45–50°F year round. This moderates the temperature of the currents of air flowing eastward across the water. Cold air is warmed, warm air is cooled. This gives us our mild, maritime climate and, if you live on the west side of the Cascade Range, our abundance of cloudy skies.

The World Was Beautiful Once

My first inkling that clouds could even be in danger of disappearing came in 1973, when I was thirteen years old and watching *Soylent Green* in a movie theater. For those of you who have not seen this classic dystopian thriller, it is set in New York City in the year 2022. The city is a post-apocalyptic wasteland, a police state ravaged by poverty, crime, corruption, and overpopulation. The sky is gray, overcast, and polluted. There are no trees, plants, or wildlife. Natural resources have been depleted. People live on squares of food presumably manufactured from soybeans, lentils, and ocean plankton. The lead characters are Thorn, a police detective, and Sol, a wise father figure. The younger Thorn knows only a ruined planet. Sol is old enough to recall when the world was beautiful, food plentiful, and nature bountiful. "The world was beautiful once," Sol reminds Thorn often.

One of the only scenes I have remembered all these years includes clouds floating over the ocean at sunset. I rented the movie recently to learn why I had found these clouds so memorable.

The clouds appear near the very end of the movie as Sol lies on his death-bed. He's listening to Beethoven's *Pastoral* Symphony and "Morning" from Grieg's *Peer Gynt Suite* while watching scenes of the beautiful world he once knew on the vast movie screen in front of him. We see what Sol sees: a meadow of flowers blowing in the breeze, deer grazing in a field, a forest, a flock of birds in flight, a cascading river, and then—after Thorn arrives—the clouds. They are low, gray, broken clouds moving in a slow, time-lapse sequence over the ocean as the sun drops below the horizon. As the sky darkens, Sol's room darkens, and the clouds appear to sweep over Sol's body.

Sol: Can you see it?

Thorn: Yes.

Sol: Isn't it beautiful?

Thorn: Oh, yes.

Sol: I told you.

Thorn: How could I know? How could I—how could I ever imagine?

I have watched this scene over and over—at least a dozen times in recent years. It has never failed to move me, to sadden me, to make me feel nostalgia for the clouds as if they were gone already.

These feelings took me by surprise. I did not expect to feel sad or to be contemplating the possibility of the end of clouds as we know them. That Earth's climate is undergoing unprecedented rapid change is no longer a matter of conjecture but documented scientific fact. Whether or not you believe these changes are natural or anthropogenic or both, we must acknowledge and address this most pressing issue facing the future of our planet. The Earth's land, water, and atmosphere are changing in profound and irreversible ways—ways that may be inimical to life.

The clouds' most important role in our climate is to produce precipitation and to modulate Earth's balance of energy. The pollutants in our atmosphere, particularly those from the burning of fossil fuels, change the chemistry of the clouds, which may impair the clouds' ability to form droplets large enough to rain. If our rain-bearing clouds (which are most of them) don't rain, this will affect the supply of fresh water, the health of natural ecosystems, and our ability to grow food, to name but a few catastrophic effects. Widespread and persistent drought is becoming more common, as are heavier rainfall events and increased flooding. Our warming oceans have already been generating more severe tropical storms, hurricanes, and flooding rains—all brought by increasing ranks of rain-bearing clouds.

These same pollutants can increase the reflectivity of clouds and increase their cooling effect on the planet. This might sound like a good thing to counter warming temperatures, but scientists are not yet able to determine if the cooling effect is offsetting the warming effect caused by the generation of the pollutants in the first place.

Scientists recently discovered from historical satellite records that the distribution of clouds across the earth has shifted toward the poles. Because less solar radiation strikes the earth at high latitudes, these clouds are not reflecting as much heat away from the planet as they would at lower, warmer latitudes.

Clouds have been described as "the wild card" and the "largest source of uncertainty" in predictions of climate change. Though the Intergovernmental Panel on Climate Change and scientists around the globe are sharpening their focus on untangling the complex feedback loops between the clouds, the atmosphere, the oceans, and landforms, the clouds are proving to be characteristically bewildering.

For millennia, humans have relied on clouds to predict the weather. It is ironic that we are just now looking to clouds to help us understand climate change and how to mitigate its negative impacts on our planet.

Nimbostratus

The Pacific Northwest has a reputation for being particularly rainy, and Nimbostratus clouds are partly to blame for this bad rap. Nimbostratus clouds are gray because they are full of raindrops, ice crystals, and snowflakes that absorb more light than they scatter. They may also be topped by other cloud layers—Altostratus, for example—that enhance the gloom. Nimbostratus clouds produce everything from a fine, mist-like rain (background rain, some locals call it) to solid, steady downpours, but they generally bring a gentler rain and usually overstay their welcome.

Nimbostratus are mid-level clouds, recall, with a base at least 6,500 feet above the ground. Until I learned this from the *Guide to the Sky* poster, I had assumed Nimbostratus were low clouds. They do appear to be low because, as my meteorologist explained to me, the bases mark the level where the ice crystals in the cloud melt and emerge from the cloud as raindrops. The actual base can be hidden not only by rainfall but also by other clouds, such as Stratocumulus, which often form beneath the Nimbostratus layer. Nimbostratus are thick, layered clouds and may extend up to 18,000 feet above their base. They can be so thick that they can hide within them well-developed Cumulus clouds. They can stretch across thousands of square miles of sky.

This book is not about weather, but what defines Nimbostratus is rain. And rain is what defines much of the Pacific Northwest. For fun, I typed "Rainy City USA" into my search engine. The first of more than five million hits? Seattle. Which is where you go for a Rain City Burger, Rain City Video, Rain City Cigar, the three-day Bumbershoot Festival or the Chance of Rain Festival, the Junior League of Seattle's *Celebrate the Rain* cookbook, and your very own "It's Always Raining in Seattle" T-shirt.

Authors of a tongue-in-cheek guide to the Pacific Northwest advise visitors to shower with their clothes on during the week prior to their arrival to acclimate themselves. Seattle is the butt of many weather jokes—"Seattleites don't tan, they rust" being a favorite. Tourist shops sell "Greetings from Seattle!" postcards; they are all gray.

Have you heard about the woman visiting Seattle for the first time? After a spate of rainy days, she asks a kid sitting at a restaurant lunch counter if it ever stopped raining. "How should I know?" he replies. "I'm only six."

No matter how much Nimbostratus clouds rain, it will never be enough to justify the "rainy city" reputations of Seattle, Olympia, or Portland. These cities are not as rainy as they are thought to be. Seattle gets a mere 37.5 inches of rain a year, Olympia 50 inches, and Portland 36 inches. The really wet places in Washington are not cities at all but remote places in the western half of the state. The uninhabited Aberdeen Reservoir, for instance, gets an average of 130.6 inches of rain a year. The small town of Forks (population 3,532 plus *Twilight* tourists) receives 119.7 inches a year, and the Humptulips Salmon Hatchery, Cougar, Naselle, Clearwater, and Grays River Hatchery slightly less. Our rainiest locations are the Hoh Rain Forest, which averages 170 inches a year, and the Sultan Basin, which gets an average of 165 inches a year.

So what's with our "rainy" cities here? The culprit, I believe, is something called "trace precipitation," which is an occurrence of less than one-hundredth of an inch of rain—just a few drops, enough to be noticed. Even this much precipitation is called "rain" and is counted in our annual total of rainy days. When you combine these days (an annual average of 157 days for Seattle) with the many cloudy days, "rainy" kind of sums it up for most people.

A pluviophile is a lover of rain, someone who finds joy and peace of mind during rainy days. You won't find the word "pluviophile" in a dictionary yet. The word appeared on the internet a few years ago—created from "pluvial," a real Latin-rooted word meaning "rainy," and "-philia," a Greek-based word root to indicate love or fondness.

"Pluviophile" is new. And it's about time. Rain is one of the best things that has ever happened to Earth. Rain not only waters plants and crops, it creates rivers and streams, nourishes rain forests, replenishes the water table, and redistributes fresh water between the oceans, land, and atmosphere. Each and every drop of rain carries with it microscopic particles—the condensation nuclei in the center of each cloud droplet in every raindrop. Rain washes these particles out of the atmosphere, which leaves the air noticeably cleaner for a time. And, by bringing these particles to the earth, rain restores nutrients to Earth. Though it may seem inconceivable that such tiny particles could make a significant difference to the richness of the soil on earth, studies have shown that they are an essential source of mineral nutrients in tropical rain forest ecosystems where rain is abundant and soils poor.

How It Rains

In the dark but not so wee hours of a February morning, I woke to the splatter of the rain on the waxy leaves of the salal outside my bedroom window. It had been raining for days—not a steady, gentle rain that might lull a person back to sleep but an erratic, loud rain, the kind that starts and stops abruptly as if someone is playing with an on-off switch.

The rain was trying to tell me something so I listened. Its rhythm brought to mind the pulsing, thrashing bands of heavy rain we'd get in Virginia at the edge of a hurricane. Thanks to the cool waters of the Pacific Ocean,

Washington is not hurricane territory. The clouds I was listening to had to be Nimbostratus and, judging by the pulsing rhythm, likely had Cumulus or even Cumulonimbus clouds embedded within. I imagined all these clouds as a flotilla of huge gray sponges full of water that squeezed out over my neighborhood, leaving dry, empty cloud-sponges in the sky.

I knew this was wrong, but I couldn't visualize what was actually happening in the clouds. I listened more carefully to the rain, and eventually my rambling mind landed on the truth: I did not know how it rained. I wasn't even sure what "it" was. There was no way for me to figure this out lying there in bed. Dr. Science was sound asleep next to me, and my bedside table held only books of light verse. In a few hours, I would slip out of bed and start my day with a cup of coffee and a stack of meteorology books to find some answers.

Nimbostratus clouds contain a mix of cloud droplets and raindrops as well as ice crystals if the tops of the clouds reach altitudes where the temperature is between 14 and 23°F. These ice crystals, which may fall as snowflakes within the cloud, become raindrops at the melting level in the cloud before they rain.

Within every Nimbostratus cloud, droplets of different sizes are rising and falling at different rates in different parts of the cloud. The cloud droplets generally range between 2 and 200 micrometers wide and are spherical; the drizzle drops are between 200 and 500 micrometers; and raindrops are typically anywhere from 500 to 5,000 micrometers, though ones as large as 8,000 micrometers (nearly a centimeter!) have been measured. Each droplet is responding to the constant force of gravity, uneven updrafts, and changing air resistance determined by their constantly changing sizes.

Not all of the droplets in a Nimbostratus fall out of the cloud as rain. A single cloud droplet remains in the cloud because it is too small and light to overcome the natural updrafts within the cloud. For such a droplet, condensation is not a direct path out of the cloud. The droplet might grow by condensation into a small raindrop, but the latent heat of condensation gives it an upward boost, which moves it away from its exit at the base of the cloud. This newly formed rain droplet could even be reduced back to a cloud droplet by evaporation.

How does a drop of water ever get out of a cloud? It has to grow heavy enough to overcome the natural updrafts beneath the cloud. I assumed that the process that initiated the formation of cloud droplets—condensation—simply continued until the cloud droplet grew heavy enough. Like the straw that broke the camel's back, I imagined there was one water vapor molecule that condensed on a large cloud droplet and sent it plummeting to earth. It turns out that condensation is a very slow process for making rain. Meteorologists estimate that it would take a solid week of condensation to produce a single raindrop. There are forces other than condensation at work inside a cloud to make raindrops. The *collision-coalescence* process is, in some ways, easier to understand than condensation. Though its name is a bit off-putting, school children would glom onto this science if it were taught as the *bumper car* process of raindrop formation.

Perhaps your childhood summer beach trips did not include an evening at the amusement park where your father and three brothers drove their bumper cars at you like maniacs. Mine did. My mom stood by and tried not to watch.

In a bumper-car rink, small, rubber-rimmed, electromagnetically powered cars zip and lurch around on a flat metal surface. If the cars all moved at the same speed, it would be an uneventful ride. Under the control of different drivers, the cars move at varying speeds and directions. Cars repeatedly collide with other cars—usually the cars driven by bigger, more aggressive drivers (fathers and older brothers, for example) would hit more cars. Sometimes they would force all the other cars onto one side of the rink and we'd all be temporarily stuck there in a clump.

Let's look at a Nimbostratus cloud, a shallow one composed solely of water droplets. This Nimbostratus cloud is the bumper-car rink, and the water droplets are the bumper cars. If all the droplets were the same size, they would have an uneventful ride through the cloud. The droplets in this cloud are of mixed sizes. As droplets fall within the cloud, the larger droplets fall faster and overtake the smaller, slower-falling droplets. Turbulence within the cloud—rising and falling air, for instance—can also cause droplets to crash into each other. This in-cloud crashing is called *collision*. After colliding, some droplets will merge together, or coalesce. This is how droplets grow large and heavy enough to fall out of the cloud as rain, though the collision-coalescence process does not necessarily guarantee that they will. Some collisions between droplets are so forceful (think whiplash in a bumper car) that the droplet breaks apart into many smaller ones, which may get caught in the cloud's updrafts. Or they might evaporate and shrink a bit and then condense and begin growing again. Every individual droplet has a unique course out of the cloud and, therefore, staggered departure times. This is why raindrops do not fall all at once as if wrung out of a sponge. Some of the droplets falling out of Nimbostratus clouds will not reach the ground but instead will evaporate in the air below the cloud base as virga.

The Nimbostratus over my house that night—the clouds that kept me awake—were launching one successful raindrop after the next. Now that I could imagine what each drop and droplet might be doing and how much work it takes each one to reach me, it is a wonder I can sleep at all on a rainy night.

The Rainbow

One of the most delightful side effects of rain is a rainbow—an optical phenomenon caused by reflection and refraction of sunlight inside falling raindrops.

Over the years of watching the clouds, I have learned when and where to find rainbows. It's a deceptively simple skill, one worth acquiring and fun to practice.

One late afternoon not long ago I was waiting at a sheltered bus stop and watching the Nimbostratus clouds break up after a day of rain. The sky had a certain quality of light I had come to associate with the appearance of rainbows. The sun was low and directly behind me so I knew a rainbow would appear in front of me. I waited for the bus. I waited for the rainbow. I chatted about the weather with a young man also waiting for the bus. I told him we might see a rainbow soon, and I pointed to the part of the sky where I guessed it would appear. In less than thirty seconds, a rainbow appeared.

The young man looked at me askance, started walking away from me, then turned his head around to say, "Lady, you're trippin' me out."

I tried to explain to him that rainbows are a common occurrence in western Washington and that if he turned his back to the sun after a rain shower he could increase his chances of seeing one.

He listened but never returned to the bus shelter, preferring instead to stand apart, a safe distance from a woman I presume he thought might turn him into a newt or a leprechaun.

Rainbows traditionally symbolize good luck, promise, hope, a bridge between Earth and paradise. Rainbows are spiritually transporting, their arcing forms seemingly capable of carrying us beyond the clouds to that place where, as the song goes, "the dreams that you dare to dream really do come true." Like dreams, rainbows and clouds are what you make of them.

Healing Clouds

During the past several years, I have engaged with the clouds mostly as a student and admirer. I have responded to the clouds emotionally on occasion. And I have wondered about the nature of my relationship to the clouds—and the relationship of human beings, of society, to the clouds. Are we paying less attention to the clouds than we used to? Are we looking up less when we are outside? What are we paying attention to when we are outside? Are our relationships to the clouds and to nature endangered? Do we understand the value of these relationships?

In 1984, Harvard biologist Edward O. Wilson published his book *Biophilia*, a seminal work of nonfiction in which he proposed that human beings have the "innate tendency to focus on life and lifelike processes." Wilson and other scientists later developed this idea into the "biophilia hypothesis," which suggests that experiencing nature supports our psychophysiological well-being.

In the same year Wilson published *Biophilia*, Roger Ulrich, a researcher in the field of health-care architecture and design, published an influential study showing that medical patients were more relaxed and healed faster in rooms featuring windows that looked onto nature—be it a landscape, sky, patch of natural scenery, or even a single tree. Further studies showed that patients in windowed rooms experienced less stress and anxiety, needed less pain medication, suffered less depression, and felt more relaxed than patients in rooms without windows. The studies looked at hospital inpatients, especially those in critical care or intensive care units, as well as outpatients undergoing dental surgery, radiation therapy, MRIs, and CAT scans. One study even included people simply in the waiting rooms of medical facilities. The research shows that the healing powers of nature are so strong that even when people experience nature vicariously through a photograph, video, or work of art, it has measurable benefits to their well-being.

And this is where the Sky Factory comes in. This small, innovative company, based in Fairfield, Iowa, manufactures virtual skylights and windows that offer a view of nature so realistic that observers respond to them as if they were looking at the real thing. Most of the illusory windows the Sky Factory makes feature a deep blue sky and, of course, clouds—almost exclusively Cirrus and Cumulus.

How realistic are the illusions? I found out firsthand one summer not long ago. Fortunately I did not have to go to a medical facility or even the Sky Factory in Iowa to do so. I just made an appointment to visit the company's traveling showroom during its tour through the Pacific Northwest.

It was hard to miss the SkyMobile. It was a 42-foot-long semi-trailer covered entirely by a photograph of a blue sky and white clouds. And it was attached to a very large white pick-up truck and parked across nine parking spaces at a shopping mall a few miles from my home.

Approaching the door at the back end of the SkyMobile, I had to wonder: was I really about to knock on a door in the sky to look at images of clouds through fake skylights?

I took a deep breath, stifled my giggles, and knocked.

The sales consultant invited me into the cool and carpeted interior of what was essentially a mobile home. I sat down on a comfortable upholstered bench and looked around. There were Cumulus humilis over the rim of the Grand Canyon out one window and modest Altocumulus clouds enhancing a sunset over the ocean out another. Through one skylight, fronds of palm trees framed a blue sky veiled with Cirrus. Through another, Cumulus fractus and Cirrus floated above the tips of Douglas firs. The clouds were realistic, the depth of the sky convincing, and each scene was framed like a real skylight or window, with wood trim, muntins, and all.

No gray Nimbostratus, no blankets of Stratus, no cauliflower-topped Cumulus or any dark clouds at all.

"I'm not seeing any bad-weather clouds," I told the salesman.

"With few exceptions," the sales consultant told me, "the Sky Factory uses Cirrus and young Cumulus—small, bright, white, nonthreatening types of clouds."

"Where were all these photos taken?" I asked.

"From all over—Nebraska, the Oklahoma panhandle, Steens Mountain in southeast Oregon, and the east side of the southern Rockies. Places with clear skies and the kinds of clouds we're looking for. The ideal photograph is a composition of blue sky and cloud in certain ratios—ones that trigger that biophilic response. We fuse the high-resolution photos onto acrylic panels an eighth of an inch thick."

The salesman showed me a section of a panel. It was hard to imagine this lightweight piece of plastic could create a convincing illusion of a real sky and real clouds.

"When these panels are installed," the salesman continued, "we recess them a few inches to enhance the perception of depth. This helps give viewers the illusion they are looking into—and not at—the sky and clouds. We also pay close attention to scale. You should see fewer clouds through a small skylight, for instance, and more but not larger clouds through a larger one. Perspective is important too. Lying on your back, you'll have a different perspective of clouds than you will from a reclined seat or an upright chair in a waiting room. We adjust the imagery to reproduce what the mind sees in order to trigger the same beneficial response as a similar view of the real sky and clouds."

It took only a few minutes of staring "through" one "window" at the "clouds" to feel transported out of the enclosed space I was in and onto a tropical beach. I could feel my eyes and mind working together as I traveled over the tops of palm trees, into the Cirrus clouds, and beyond to the blue sky. I wasn't merely looking at a pleasing photograph. The illusion of being drawn through several miles of atmosphere had engaged me in a deeper, more visceral way.

Just before I left, the sales consultant told me a story from a cancer-care clinic in Indiana where the Sky Factory had installed a four-by-six-foot illusory skylight in a waiting room. One patient returned to the waiting room every day after his treatments to sit under the skylight. When a nurse told him he could go home, the patient said, "I know I can, but is it okay to sit here for a while? It has such a wonderful, spiritual feeling."

I was glad these indoor clouds could be so comforting for those who truly needed them. Whether illusory or real, merely distracting or powerfully engaging, the clouds often arrive just when you need them most.

A week after my mother died, I felt the true weight of my grief after I returned home to Olympia. I spent the better part of most days sitting around staring at the walls, unable to feel much of anything but loss. It felt wrong somehow to go outside that June to feel the joy in the summer days, the trees, the rhododendron and azalea in full bloom, even the sun's warmth. Eventually I decided I would feel closer to my mother in my garden than in my living room, so one morning I moved a lawn chair into the front yard and positioned it in the most Eden-like spot I could find. It didn't take long to notice the clouds.

They appeared, as if summoned, from behind me. They were Cumulus fractus, the bright and spritely ones. The way my chair was facing, the clouds appeared from behind me and swept across the sky in front of me. This created the illusion that they were flying out of the top of my head. I decided to take advantage of this illusion to see if the clouds might sweep away some of my sadness. Without any experience or set of instructions for accomplishing this, I just started following the clouds with my eyes, from the moment they appeared in my field of vision to the moment I lost sight of them. I began to feel relaxed, and then gradually I sensed some strange lightening of my heavy heart and depressed mind. Rather than dismiss the sensation as nonsense, I accepted it and kept my eyes on the sky. The clouds kept coming. Cloud by cloud my grief, apparently held in some form the clouds could absorb, diminished a little bit that day.

In the weeks and months following my first cloud therapy, I realized that my relationship to the clouds had undergone a profound change. I really needed them. This was not what I had expected would come from my life with the clouds. When that life started, the clouds were merely beautiful objects and the subject of my curiosity. Soon they became an obsession, a personal challenge, the exacting designer of my learning curve. For the longest while, the clouds were always "them," and I was always "me." They were always doing their dynamic cloudy things and I was always running, lead-footed, trying to keep up with them. I felt peeved that they wouldn't slow down or ever help me out. But after they came to my rescue when I was in a state of grief, I felt indebted to them as if they were living things, good friends and soul mates.

EPILOGUE

Beneath the lake where I swim is an aquifer—a natural store of water that moves underground through sand, rock, and gravel. Because there are cracks in the rock beneath the lake, some of that water flows into the lake through cold, underground springs. And because there are no surface outlets—no little streams or creeks flowing in or out—the water in the lake is trapped in the lake. The only escape is through surface evaporation.

As I floated on my back in the lake one afternoon, as I often do in the summer, it was easy to forget that I was in water. I was submerged but floating. The only sensation of water was where it lapped at the outer edges of my face and my shoulders.

Because I was thinking about the aquifer, it was not long before I began imagining that I too was evaporating, disappearing into the sky to join the clouds. They were Cumulus clouds, the humble, comfortable-looking ones. From where I was floating, I could see these clouds in the blue sky and also their patchy, wave-wrinkled reflections on the surface of the dark lake.

The clouds drifted slowly over the trees on the western shore. I turned my body so that I was aligned with the clouds, my toes pointing west.

Seventy percent of the earth is covered by clouds at any given time.

Seventy-one percent of the earth's surface is covered by water.

Sixty-five percent of the human body is water.

I imagined the water evaporating off the surface of the lake and the molecules of water in my skin following along, rising into the air. Could I ever reach a cloud this way—that one there or that one? Or would the clouds build and rain themselves down on me first? Perhaps we could all meet somewhere in the middle.

Although there was a mile or so of atmosphere between us, I felt a special kinship with these clouds at the lake. There was so little difference between us.

Here we were, fluid bodies floating.

Here were the clouds, aloft, reflected.

Here I was, afloat, reflecting.

I had found my way in.

GENERAL SOURCES

Ahrens, Donald C. *Meteorology Today*, 8th edition. Belmont, CA: Thomson Brooks/ Cole, 2007.

Allaby, Michael. *Encyclopedia of Weather and Climate*. New York: Facts On File, 2002.

Cole, K. C. *First You Build a Cloud: And Other Reflections on Physics as a Way of Life*. New York: Harcourt, Brace, and Company, 1999.

Day, John A., and Vincent J. Schaefer. *Peterson First Guides to Clouds and Weather*. Boston: Houghton-Mifflin, 1991.

Gedzelman, Stanley David. *The Science and Wonders of the Atmosphere*. New York: John Wiley & Sons, 1980.

Hamblyn, Richard. *The Invention of Clouds: How an Amateur Meteorologist Forged the Language of the Skies*. New York: Picador, 2002.

————. *The Met Office Pocket Cloud Book*. Cincinnati, OH: David and Charles, 2010.

Laskin, David. *Rains All the Time: A Connoisseur's History of Weather in the Pacific Northwest*. Seattle: Sasquatch Books, 1997.

Ludlum, David M. *Audubon Society Field Guide to North American Weather*. New York: Alfred A. Knopf, 1991.

Mass, Cliff. *The Weather of the Pacific Northwest*. Seattle: University of Washington Press, 2008.

Merriam-Webster's, Inc. *Webster's New Collegiate Dictionary*, 9th edition. Springfield, MA: G. & C. Merriam Company, 1980.

Oxford University Press. *The Compact Edition of the Oxford English Dictionary*. Complete text reproduced micrographically. Oxford, England: Oxford University Press, 1971.

————. *Oxford English Dictionary Online.* Oxford, England: Oxford University Press. December 2016. www.oed.com.

Pretor-Pinney, Gavin. *The Cloudspotter's Guide: The Science, History, and Culture of Clouds.* New York: Perigee, 2006.

Suchocki, John. *Conceptual Chemistry: Understanding Our World of Atoms and Molecules,* 4th edition. Upper Saddle River, NJ: Prentice Hall, 2011.

World Meteorological Organization. *International Cloud Atlas: Manual on the Observation of Clouds and Other Meteors* (WMO-No.407). Geneva, Switzerland: World Meteorological Organization, 2017. The new web-based edition (and past editions) can be accessed at www.wmocloudatlas.org.

NOTES

Prologue

A Guide to the Sky, by Art Rangno. Seattle, WA. 2000. This eighth edition is out
   of print, but a later and equally inspiring edition is available (at widely varying
   prices) through Art Rangno's website www.cloud-maven.com.

"Pineapple Express" is the name for storms that travel from north of Hawaii to
   the West Coast. These storms are but one expression of the currents of water
   vapor transported horizontally from the tropics and subtropics and, because they
   occur globally, are increasingly referred to by meteorologists as "atmospheric rivers." Atmospheric rivers are often associated with strong winds, heavy rains, and
   flooding.

Cloud

SkyWarn Weather Spotter training courses are offered across the US, http://skywarn
   .org/skywarn-training/ (accessed April 2017).

"Danger Zone" written by Giorgio Moroder, Kenny Loggins, Tom Whitlock. Lyrics
   © Sony/TV Music Publishing LLC, Warner/Chappell Music, Inc.

"According to the National Weather Service . . ." Cloud cover terminology and
   definitions are from the National Weather Service. www.weather.gov/bgm
   /forecast_terms (accessed February 2017).

According to the National Weather Service . . ." Rainfall in Olympia, WA, and Miami, FL, is from US Climate Data, www.usclimatedata.com and the Western Regional Climate Center www.wrcc.dri.edu/climatedata/tables/ (accessed February 2017).

The Invention of Clouds: How an Amateur Meteorologist Forged the Language of the Skies, by Richard Hamblyn. New York, NY: Picador, 2002.

That Robert Hooke "hurried from one inquiry to another with brilliant but inconclusive results" is from *Dictionary of National Biography*, Vol. 27, Lee Sydney, ed. London: Smith, Elder, 1891 as quoted in Hamblyn, p. 98.

"Over the next several decades, meteorologists modified . . ." The 1975 edition of the *International Cloud Atlas* (Volume 1) includes the prefaces of the 1939 and 1956 editions, which provide interesting details on the challenging work of publishing cloud classifications over the centuries. A pdf of the 1975 edition is available under the "Links" tab at www.wmo-cloudatlas.org (accessed February 2017).

"I found my way to the Cloud Appreciation Society website . . ." The website is https://cloudappreciationsociety.org (accessed April 2017).

"One of the newest supplementary features to be named . . ." The story of the asperitas is recounted by the founder of the Cloud Appreciation Society, Gavin Pretor-Pinney, in his blog and delightful Google Zeitgest talk. Both are posted on the Cloud Appreciation Society website, cloudappreciationsociety.org/july-2015/ (accessed April 2017).

"Because the Latin names can be unwieldy . . ." The alphanumeric codes for cloud cover appear on the National Weather Service's website, www.weather.gov/images/wrh/Metar_cloud_legend.png. Though not included in this list, the codes for Towering Cumulus (TCU), Cumulonimbus (CB), and also Altocumulus castellanus (ACC) appear in Terminal Aerodrome (TAF) and Meteorological Aerodrome Report (METAR) codes published by NOAA/NWS and are used primarily in aviation.

"Surprisingly, the most helpful book I found . . ." *The Art of Bird Identification*, by Pete Dunne. Mechanicsburg, PA: Stackpole Books, 2012.

Visible

"There are plenty of books on the art of seeing . . ." *Art Objects: Essays in Ecstasy and Effrontery*, by Jeannette Winterson. New York, NY: Vintage International, 1997 pp. 8–10. In the title, "Art" is a noun, not an adjective; "Objects" is a verb, not a noun.

"What distinguishing features enable us to identify Stratus clouds?" *The Science and Wonder of the Atmosphere*, by Stanley Gedzelman. p. 31.

"Pogonip." *Merriam-Webster.com*. Merriam-Webster, n.d. www.merriam-webster.com /dictionary/pogonip (accessed February 2017).

"This benign and naturally occurring fog turned toxic . . ." "The Great Smog" by Devra Davis in *History Today*. 52, no. 12 (December 2002). www .historytoday.com/devra-davis/great-smog (accessed April 2017).

"killed an estimated twelve thousand people . . ." "A Retrospective Assessment of Mortality from the London Smog Episode of 1952: The Role of Influenza and Pollution," by Michelle L. Belle, Devra L. Davis, Tony Fletcher in *Environmental Health Perspectives*, 112, no. 1 (January 2004).

"Naturally occurring fogs can also prove menacing . . ." California's fog detection and warning system is described in "Best Practices for Road Weather Management, Version 3.0" by Ray Murphy et al. Washington, DC: US Department of Transportation, Federal Highway Administration, June 2012, pp. 15–18. Ironically, the California Department of Transportation has not been able to assess the effectiveness of the system due to a decline in tule fogs as reported in "Loathed by Motorists, Loved by Fruit Trees, California's Tule Fog Fades Away," by Marianne Lavelle in *The Daily Climate* (May 22, 2014). www.dailyclimate.org /tdc-newsroom/2014/05/tule-fog-decline (accessed March 2017).

"Caribou fog . . ." *Meteorology Today*, by Donald Ahrens, p. 114.

"Cape Disappointment . . . is ranked as one of the foggiest places . . ." *The Weather of the Pacific Northwest*, by Cliff Mass, p. 6.

Mass

"According to one estimate . . ." *The Stories Clouds Tell Us*, by Margaret A. LeMone. Washington, DC: American Meteorological Society, 2008, p. 1.

"carbon dioxide (CO_2) at just 0.04 percent . . ." Though this concentration seems miniscule, the level of carbon dioxide in our air has risen 20 percent since it was first measured in 1958. This increase has been linked to climate change, specifically to global warming. The amount of carbon dioxide is usually described in parts per million (ppm), which is the number of molecules per every million air molecules. The average global level of CO_2 in the atmosphere passed 400 ppm in early 2017.

"Those are awful pictures . . . ." Personal communication, William Cotton, meteorologist and professor emeritus, Department of Atmospheric Sciences, Colorado State University, and author (with R.A. Anthes) of *Storm and Cloud Dynamics (International Geophysics Series)*, 2nd edition. San Diego: Academic Press, 2011.

"While Genesis does not mention . . ." Scholarly interpretations of Genesis 1:7 can be accessed online at Bible Hub, http://biblehub.com/genesis/1-7.htm (accessed April 2017).

Illustration of modeled thermals from Chin-Hoh Moeng "Large-Eddy Simulation of a Stratus-Topped Boundary Layer. Part I: Structure and Budgets" in *Journal of Atmospheric Sciences*, 43, no. 23 (1986). Used with permission.

Lofty Hermitage in Cloudy Mountains, ink on paper, by Fan Fanghu. 14th century Chinese, Honolulu Academy of Arts. Source: Wikimedia Commons.

The Mustard Seed Garden Manual of Painting, Mai-Mai Sze, translator and editor. Princeton, NJ: Princeton University Press, 1978, p. 129. (This is the facsimile of the 1887–1888 Shanghai edition.)

Water

"In the still images, vapor appears . . ." The National Weather Service features vapor images of the United States from Geostationary Operational Environment Satellite (GOES) system on their website, www.weather.gov/satellite#wv (accessed May 2017). Select the "24 Hours" loop to animate the images. (Searching on "water vapor imagery" on YouTube will yield many mesmerizing month- and year-long GOES loops.)

Droplets

Science from Your Airplane Window, by Elizabeth A. Wood. New York: Dover Publications, 1975, pp. 68–69 and inside front cover. (The original edition was published in 1968 by Houghton-Mifflin).

"I reached out to the Outreach Program . . ." Jack Scheff, K–12 Outreach Coordinator (2010–2013), University of Washington, Department of Atmospheric Sciences, www.atmos.washington.edu/~outreach. The information in this section is based on interviews and emails between 2010 and 2016, during which time Scheff earned his MS (2011) and PhD (2014) in Atmospheric Sciences at the University of Washington.

"I was over my head, and not even Richard Feynman . . ." One of Feynman's most accessible books for the general reader is his 1984 autobiographical *"Surely You're Joking, Mr. Feynman!": Adventures of a Curious Character* (New York: W.W. Norton & Company, Inc. 1997). More challenging is *QED: The Strange Theory of Light and Matter* (Princeton, NJ: Princeton University Press, 1985) and *Six Easy Pieces: Essentials of Physics Explained by Its Most Brilliant Teacher* (Reading, MA: Helix Books, 1995). I would not recommend non-physics majors attempt *The Feynman*

Lectures on Physics. Vol. 1. (New York: Basic Books, 2010) in which Feynman addresses the scattering of light.

" . . . a physics major working on a graduate degree in atmospheric sciences . . ." The conversation in this section is based on my interviews and email correspondence with Nathan Steiger between 2012 and 2016 during which time Steiger earned both his MS (2013) and PhD (2015) in Atmospheric Sciences at the University of Washington.

Clouds in a Glass of Beer: Simple Experiments in Atmospheric Physic, by Craig Bohren. Minneola, NY: Dover Publications, 2001. This is a reprint of the 1987 edition published by John Wiley & Sons, New York.

"I sent Dr. Bohren an email . . ." This section is based on a series of emails from Dr. Bohren in 2016.

"Researchers at the University of Music and Performing Arts in Vienna . . ." Alexander Mayer, et al. "Analysis of bow-hair fibres" in *International Symposium on Musical Acoustics, Program and Abstracts of ISMA 2007*, Barcelona, Spain. Ed. Joaquim Agulló, Institut d'Estudis Catalans. www.fineviolinbows.com/pdf/Analysis _bowhair.pdf (accessed April 2017).

"When the clouds come out . . ." "How to Shoot for Every Type of Cloud Cover." David Johnston. Photography Roundtable 9/17/2014 blog http://photography roundtable.com/1365/shoot-every-type-cloud-cover/ (accessed March 2017).

"Clouds are great for all detail shots . . ." David Johnston, email communication.

Ice

"my older son had left his college chemistry book at home . . ." *Conceptual Chemistry: Understanding Our World of Atoms and Molecules*, 4th edition, by John Suchocki. (This is an excellent book for those needing a refresher of high-school chemistry. A 5th edition was published in 2013.)

"Kaolinite: Mineral Information," Minerology Database, Hudson School of Minerology, www.mindat.org/min-2156.html (accessed February 2017).

The temperature and altitude of kaolinite in the atmosphere provided by Art Rangno, personal communication.

Crystals

Illustration of "Types of Frozen Precipitation." Vincent Schaefer Papers, Special Collections & Archives, University at Albany, SUNY.

"How Do You Like Your Skies Natural or Manmade?" is a PowerPoint presentation by Rosalind Peterson and Todd Blackmon posted on the website of the Agriculture

Defense Coalition, http://agriculturedefensecoalition.org/content/geoengineering -current-actions (accessed February 2017).

" . . . Since World War II, the U.S. government has been experimenting . . ." *Weather Matters: An American Cultural History Since 1900*, by Bernard Mergen. Lawrence, KS: University of Kansas Press, 2008, pp. 117–118.

"None of these cloud-seeding experiments . . ." Art Rangno, personal communication. The list of and links to Art Rangno's published articles and critiques can be found on his website, www.cloud-maven.com.

Suspended

The Man Who Rode the Thunder, by William H. Rankin. New York: Pyramid Books, 1961 (original edition published by Prentice-Hall, 1960).

Atmosphere

The Discovery of a World in the Moone, by John Wilkins. London: Printed by E.G. for Michael Sparke and Edward Forrest, 1638. Digitized edition of the original text by archives.org and available for free download at https://archive.org/details /discoveryofworld00wilk (accessed April 2017).

"Where did all the oxygen come from?" *An Ocean of Air: Why the Wind Blows and Other Mysteries of the Atmosphere*. New York: Harcourt, 2007, pp. 44–47. And "The Earth's first breathable atmosphere," by Shireen Gonzaga in *Earth*, March 2, 2011. http://earthsky.org/earth/the-earths-first-breathable-atmosphere (accessed April 2017).

"Other theories point to Jupiter . . ." "Nitrogen on Jupiter: A deep atmospheric source," by Ronald G. Prinn and Eduardo P. Olaguer in *Journal of Geophysical Research*, Vol. 86, Issue C10, October 20, 1981. Online provider John Wiley & Sons, (accessed January 2017).

"Air pressure is the force . . ." *Eyewitness Weather*, by Brian Cosgrove. New York, NY: DK Publishing, 2007, p. 70.

"Atmospheric pressure is simply the weight of air . . ." *Wild About Weather*, by Ed Brotak. New York: Lark Books, p. 26.

"Because air is a fluid . . . *The Atmosphere: Planetary Heat Engine*, by Gregory Vogt. Minneapolis, MN: Twenty-First Century Books, 1873, p. 14.

"Air pressure is the weight of air pressing down on the earth . . ." *National Audubon Society First Field Guide: Weather*, by Jonathan D.W. Kahl. New York, NY: Scholastic, p. 150.

"Pressure is a force . . ." Vogt, p. 13.

"High pressure areas . . ." Brotak, p. 33.

"Atmospheric pressure is the weight . . ." *Weather*, by Eduardo Banquieri. Brooklyn, NY: Enchanted Lion Books, 2006, p. 12.

"Think of air as a three-dimensional pool table . . ." Vogt, p. 13.

"It's the only thing I remember . . ." *Meteorology: An Introduction to the Wonders of the Weather*, by Robert G. Fovell. Chantilly, VA: The Teaching Company (The Great Courses), 2010.

The Essential Cosmic Perspective, 5th edition, by Jeffrey Bennett et al. San Francisco: Pearson, 2009.

"NASA Scientists Find 'Impossible' Cloud on Titan—Again," by Elizabeth Zubritsky on website of National Aeronautics and Space Administration. Sept. 20, 2016, www.nasa.gov/feature/goddard/2016/nasa-scientists-find-impossible-cloud-on-titan-again (accessed March 2017).

"Scientists estimate that these clouds cover . . ." "Review: Stratocumulus Clouds," by Robert Wood in *Monthly Weather Review*, Volume 140, No. 8. American Meteorological Society, August 2012. http://journals.ametsoc.org/doi/full/10.1175/MWR-D-11-00121.1 (accessed April 2017).

Above

"Many people know this cloud formation as 'mackerel skies' . . ." Depending on which meteorologist, field guide, or textbook you consult, you may find Altocumulus clouds also called "mackerel skies."

"He had stretched out his bare feet . . ." *Second Harvest*, by Jean Giono. London: Harvill Press, 1999, p. 25. (First published in 1930 with the title *Regain*).

Earth

Soylent Green. Harry Harrison (screenplay), Richard Fleischer (director). Metro-Goldwyn-Mayer, 1973. Warner Home Video, 2006 (DVD).

"The pollutants in our atmosphere . . ." "Clouds and Radiation," by Steve Graham. Earth Observatory website of National Aeronautics and Space Administration, http://earthobservatory.nasa.gov/Features/Clouds/ (accessed August 2016).

"Scientists recently discovered . . ." "Expanding Tropics Push High Altitude Clouds Toward Poles" by Ellen Gray. May 15, 2016. National Aeronautics and Space Administration (NASA) website, www.nasa.gov/feature/goddard/2016/expanding-tropics-pushing-high-altitude-clouds-towards-poles (accessed June 2016).

"Clouds have been described as 'the wild card' . . ." "Clouds: The Wild Card of Climate Change." Arlington, VA: National Science Foundation website, www.nsf .gov/news/special_reports/clouds/question.jsp (accessed May 2016).

"Authors of a tongue-in-cheek guidebook . . ." *Northwest Basic Training: Essential Skills for Visitors, Newcomers, and Native Northwesterners* by Greg Eiden and Kurt D. Hollomon. Seattle: Sasquatch Books, 2001, p. 1.

"These cities are not as rainy as they are thought to be . . ." Rainfall data from the University of Washington Department of Atmospheric Sciences, www.atmos .washington.edu/marka/normals/wa.normals.2010.html (accessed December 2016).

Biophilia, by Edward O. Wilson. Cambridge, MA: Harvard University Press, 1984.

The Biolphilia Hypothesis, Stephen R. Kellert and Edward O. Wilson, eds., Washington, DC: Island Press, 1993.

"View through a Window May Influence Recovery from Surgery," by Roger Ulrich, in *Science*, 224, no. 4647 (April 27, 1984).

GRATITUDE

Lovely, generous, and inspiring—such are the clouds and the many people who contributed to the creation of this book.

First and foremost, thanks to my meteorologist, Art Rangno, for his *Guide to the Sky* posters; for nine years of unstinting guidance, hundreds of explanations, diagrams, and stunning and illustrative photographs of clouds over Arizona; and for unwavering encouragement and sense of humor. The clouds are lucky to have Art as their champion.

For expertise, data, and manuscript review, thanks to meteorologists William Cotton, Jeff Renner, Mark Albright, and Craig Bohren. For their patience explaining the subatomic life of a cloud, I am grateful to the enthusiastic and patient Jack Scheff and Nathan Steiger, formerly of the University of Washington's Department of Atmospheric Sciences in Seattle.

For camaraderie, inspiration, and solace, thanks to fellow writers in Olympia—storm-tossed John Dodge; wind-swept Jim Lynch; and pre-dawn scribe of the natural world, Anne Kilgannon; in Virginia, thanks to Marietta McCarty—kin and friend. For the bike rides and tireless teaching, thanks to Maxine Dunkelman. For the big-view office space, stand-up desk, and jars of gray, white, and blue jelly beans arranged into cloud formations, thanks to Jodi Backlund and Manek Mistry. Thanks to artist Anita Ellison and her watercolor students at the Olympia Center. For manuscript reading and critique, thanks to Kevin Ingram, Roger Mudd, Amy Osowksi, Tim Osowski, and Cathy Williams. Thanks to the sixty-seven people who participated in my 2010 Cloud Survey with honesty and humor and to all those who sent me cloud pictures from afar or called to alert me to beautiful and strange clouds passing over Olympia.

Working with Mountaineers Books has kept me aloft on Cloud Nine for the past several years. Deepest gratitude to Kate Rogers, Mary Metz, Jen Grable, and the rest of the enthusiastic, supportive, creative staff in Seattle, as well as fabulous freelance editors Kirsten Colton and Chris Dodge.

And finally, to my husband, Mike "Dr. Science" Ruth and our two sons, Will and Nelson, for their abiding support during my journey into the clouds. I love you all more than anything in the sky.

INDEX

ABOUT THE AUTHOR

Michael D. Ruth

Maria Mudd Ruth is the author of more than a dozen books on natural history topics for children and adults. Her most recent book, *Rare Bird: Pursuing the Mystery of the Marbled Murrelet,* was reissued in paperback by Mountaineers Books in 2013. Though much easier to find than a small, elusive seabird nesting in the old-growth forest, the clouds proved as challenging to study, as mysterious to understand, and as joyful to behold. Maria lives in Olympia, Washington. For more information on her work, visit her website at www.mariaruthbooks.net.

recreation • lifestyle • conservation

MOUNTAINEERS BOOKS is a leading publisher of mountaineering literature and guides—including our flagship title, *Mountaineering: The Freedom of the Hills*—as well as adventure narratives, natural history, and general outdoor recreation. Through our two imprints, Skipstone and Braided River, we also publish titles on sustainability and conservation. We are committed to supporting the environmental and educational goals of our organization by providing expert information on human-powered adventure, sustainable practices at home and on the trail, and preservation of wilderness.

The Mountaineers, founded in 1906, is a 501(c)(3) nonprofit outdoor activity and conservation organization whose mission is "to explore, study, preserve, and enjoy the natural beauty of the outdoors." One of the largest such organizations in the United States, it sponsors classes and year-round outdoor activities throughout the Pacific Northwest, including climbing, hiking, backcountry skiing, snowshoeing, bicycling, camping, paddling, and more. The Mountaineers also supports its mission through its publishing division, Mountaineers Books, and promotes environmental education and citizen engagement. For more information, visit The Mountaineers Program Center, 7700 Sand Point Way NE, Seattle, WA 98115-3996; phone 206-521-6001; www.mountaineers.org; or email info@mountaineers.org.

Our publications are made possible through the generosity of donors and through sales of more than 800 titles on outdoor recreation, sustainable lifestyle, and conservation. To donate, purchase books, or learn more, visit us online.

MOUNTAINEERS BOOKS
1001 SW Klickitat Way, Suite 201 • Seattle, WA 98134
800-553-4453 • mbooks@mountaineersbooks.org • www.mountaineersbooks.org